THE AMAZING GRAYS TRILOGY

The heartbeat of the author's personal Journey of Joy is God's amazing grace. Relationship with horses and the following scriptures inspired each title in the trilogy:

Amazing Grays, Amazing Grace:

> *"Enter by the narrow gate; for wide is the gate and broad is the way that leads to destruction and there are many who go in by it. Because narrow is the gate and difficult is the way which leads to life, and there are few who find it. – Matthew 7:13-14*

He Came Looking for Me:

> *"In My Father's house are many mansions; if it were not so I would have told you. I go to prepare a place for you." – John 14:2*

Discipleship with Horses:

> *" I delight to do Thy will, O God." – Psalm 40:8*

DISCIPLESHIP
WITH HORSES

Journey of Joy

Lynn Baber

Discipleship with Horses

Photographs courtesy of: Karen Mitchell Smith, Brianna Dunn, Kalena Randall, Shirley Cook, Mendi Hartung.

Published by Ark Press 2014
ISBN 978-1-938836-08-4

AUTHOR'S NOTE:

"To whom much is given, from him much will be required."
– Luke 12:48

God has allowed me to spend decades in the company of my equally-yoked husband – and horses. The road I traveled before wasn't always joyful, but God in His faithfulness revealed that I was never alone and He was simply preparing me for what was just over the hill.

Focus and commitment are requirements of worthy leadership and building faith. Horses teach me the full measure of both, helping me to appreciate the limitless grace and love of my Savior, Jesus Christ.

Halfway through the writing process of *Journey of Joy* I realized it was the final book in a trilogy that began with *Amazing Grays, Amazing Grace* five years ago. Bo and Swizzle, two gray quarter horses, initiated this particular journey with me, and Shiner and Ace kept it going.

Amazing Grays, Amazing Grace introduces the gospel link between the Bible and the barn and "the promise He has promised us – eternal life" (1 John 2:25).

He Came Looking for Me is the true story of Shiner's rescue that proves God's promise is true, for horses and for every child of the King of Kings.

Discipleship with Horses is an inspirational and practical book to help you claim Jesus' promise of peace, joy, and freedom from fear today. As these tools build your horse's faith in you, your own faith in Christ will expand.

Christian Horse Training (CHT) is the way I share the truth and practical application of God's grace, mercy, and faithfulness with other horsemen and horsewomen who love Jesus. The purpose of discipleship with horses is to equip them to do likewise on their own journey of faith.

Christian Horse Training isn't about training horses, but helping Christians find joy in their own journey with God, horses, and one another.

I no longer accept horses in training and the ministry does not charge for CHT events. No blessing is complete until it is passed along to others. Through *Discipleship with Horses - Journey of Joy*, I hope to pass the gift on to you so you can keep it going.

It's been quite a ride. Would you expect anything less from the God who spoke the world into existence?

Will you ride with me?

Shiner and Me

TABLE OF CONTENTS

WHAT IS THE JOURNEY OF JOY?

Success is the quality of the journey that begins with submission to God's will and continues until His will becomes our joy. There is a world of difference between:

"O My Father, if it is possible, let this cup pass from Me; nevertheless, not as I will, but as You will."
– Matthew 26:39

and,

" I delight to do Thy will, O God." – Psalm 40:8

The beginning of the journey recognizes and accepts God's choice above our own, but it is a conscious decision of submission, capitulation, and resignation that subjugates a personal preference for a different circumstance by yielding to the will of God.

Horses begin training by accepting the will of the trainer over their own preference to laze in the pasture with herd buddies. They often submit, capitulate, and are resigned to the greater power of the trainer. Horses may offer obedience, but it is a conscious decision each one makes to yield to the new boss.

The most important predictors of relationship success are

the amount of time spent together and the degree of focus each party places on the other. The process of sanctification, the personal journey with Christ, starts with commitment and continues by:

- Prayer
- Bible study
- Discussion
- Teaching
- Application
- Works as the natural fruit of faith
- Fellowship with Christ and others in the family

The process of transformative relationship with a horse also begins with commitment and continues with:

- Liberty work
- Ground exercises/games
- Pasture or stall visits just "because"
- Pursuing challenges designed to reveal weaknesses in faith
- Obstacles
- Teaching
- Practice
- Fellowship with Christ and other members of His body in the equine community

Discipleship with horses is the subject and heart of Christian Horse Training (CHT). The foundation of both sanctification and CHT is God's Word in the person of Jesus Christ and the living Word of scripture. CHT is not a facility or a scripted lesson plan. CHT is a lifestyle of commitment.

Specific routines or repetitive "games" that work for some

trainers are not the lifeblood of CHT and do not necessarily produce transformative relationship. Simple routine and repetition of a particular exercise more predictably create a habit of task than a habit of obedience. The secret of relationship is not **what** is done, but **how**, **why**, and **by whom** it is done.

Discipleship with horses describes, teaches, and shares how the same principles of your journey of joy with Jesus Christ can be used to offer leadership to a horse to bring it into delightful and confidant fellowship with you, a worthy master. Gospel messages are the foundation of CHT.

Christian Horse Training (CHT) offers horses relationship that transforms conscious capitulation into reflexive, instinctive obedience built upon faith in a worthy leader.

Delight in God's will does not recognize any conscious decision to obey or preference of outcome apart from God's plan. When His will becomes your will, delight and faith abound.

The journey of joy you share with Jesus - and with your horse – can be effortless. Every load becomes so light it fails to even register as a burden. What could be more blessed than to walk each day in true delight?

Will you ride with me on this Journey of Joy?

> *"You will show me the path of life; In Your presence is fullness of joy." – Psalm 16:11*

Enough is as Good as a Feast

One simple truth about commitment and its effect on the quality of human lives hinges on the idea of *enough;* of contentment, of joy in the journey. This simple truth, embodied in the title of this section, is a totally foreign concept to populations and generations who are more focused on the acquisition of fame, fortune, and an ever-expanding base of friends on Facebook than relationships held together with bonds forged by commitment, time spent together, and shared experience.

How much money is enough? How many Facebook friends are enough? How many pairs of shoes are enough? How many hits on your latest YouTube video are enough? These questions would stymie some adults and most young folks. The concept of *enough* might cause others consternation, but at least older folks might understand the questions.

> *"He who loves silver will not be satisfied with silver;*
> *Nor he who loves abundance, with increase.*
> *This also is vanity." - Ecclesiastes 5:10*

What would happen if we changed the subject from the acquisition of things and focused instead on the issue of relationship? How many people are content with their spouse, children, boss, minister, friends, dog, or horse?

Who among us hasn't hoped for something better than we presently have?

For example:

- My husband doesn't tell me he loves me anymore. Maybe if I give him the cold shoulder he'll think that I don't care about him either.
- My wife spends too much time at work. Maybe if I work late for a week or two she'll get a taste of what it's like to come home to an empty house.
- My son is going through a rebellious stage and won't study, do his chores, or pay attention when I speak to him. Maybe he'll grow out of it.
- My daughter's friends are not good influences. Maybe when she changes schools next year…
- My horse is getting really pushy at feeding time. Maybe if I hold the bucket out in front of me and carry a whip he'll stay out of my way.
- My horse is really spooky. Last week something scared him and he knocked me to the ground when he spun around. Maybe if I stay on this side of the fence…
- I can't get my horse to stop. I say "Whoa" and pull back on the reins but he's just so hard mouthed and stubborn. Maybe I need to get a correction bit.
- Maybe I should get a better horse…
- Maybe I should get a better husband… wife…
- Maybe we should have another child who might listen to us…
- I don't have as much faith in Jesus Christ as everyone else at church seems to have. Maybe I need to get a better God…

The most profound and beautiful relationships are built on what seem like small, simple, insignificant things.

> *"These small and perishable bodies we now have were given to us as ponies are given to schoolboys. We must learn to manage: not that we may someday be free of horses altogether but that someday we may ride bareback, confident and rejoicing, those greater mounts, those winged, shining and world-shaking horses which perhaps even now expect us with impatience, pawing and snorting in the King's stables. Not that the gallop would be of any value unless it were a gallop with the King; but how else - since He has retained His own charger - should we accompany Him."* - C.S. Lewis

Those in right relationship and the most worthy of leaders do not aspire to be either right or worthy. They simply are. The cobblestones, bricks, blocks, and footings of relationship add up over days, weeks, and years to form what is amazing, inspirational, and in some ways even supernatural.

Do you find fulfillment in the quiet times spent alone with your horse? With your spouse? With Jesus? Would your horse still have a secure home if you decided to stop competing? Are successes enough even when no one else notices? If not, why aren't these tiny times enough?

One uniquely human characteristic is the ability to turn a dream fulfilled into a disappointment rather than a delight. Some girls hope that one day a pony will jog into their yard and get to stay. Imagine the delight when that girl finally

owns her own horse. A new world opens and a dream is realized.

Fast forward a few years and that horse may still be cherished. But for some, the equine answer to prayer becomes a point of discontent if it isn't fast enough, tall enough, smart enough, obedient enough, or competitive enough to suit the now older girl. The prayer was answered, the dream delivered, but it wasn't enough.

The same is true for young marrieds who dream of owning their own small home. They scrimp and save and finally get the keys to a house that needs just a little paint and repair to make it the hoped for castle. Should they begin to compare their little slice of heaven with the larger and more updated homes of friends or family the dream starts to lose its luster. Discontent replaces a dream fulfilled.

How many people do you know who are never satisfied?

Marriages often fail when daily routine and real life tarnish the image of bride and groom in the wedding album. The secret to happiness, contentment, delight, and relationship is valuing what you have today.

The End of a New Dream

Before my right knee was replaced with a hunk of titanium I budgeted upright activity to just two hours a day. That included household chores, work, entertainment, personal hygiene, and horse activities. Needless to say, it seemed as if my days of riding horses were quickly coming to an end. That was okay, I had many wonderful years and was content.

After eight sleepless months, I folded. This had been coming since 1980. My horse career itself was something of a miracle. Back in the mid-1990's a surgeon looked at the X-ray on his viewing screen and said, "What did you say you do again?" I rattled off my daily routine of starting colts, breeding and showing stallions, hauling feed, and everything else that goes with training horses. He replied, "That's impossible. With a knee like that you can't." The only explanation is that God had a plan.

I wanted to go out with all my original equipment but pain finally beat me and I had the knee replaced. The surgery and recovery was a success and I started to ride again. I began to look forward to really *training* and maybe even competing at something fun and challenging. My dreams started taking shape and expanded in scope with each hour under saddle.

First ride with my new knee. - Bo

Then I began to realize that the new knee would not give me back as much as I initially thought. I could ride. I could train. I could work - but not hours and hours on end as I used to and was planning to once again. After all, it takes a lot of time to train six mature horses when only one has a clue what that means.

First to go was the dream of competition. The next item off the list was my plan to get all six horses trained to the standards I used to apply. Yet I wasn't disappointed, I was thrilled. Why?

I can still ride with purpose! I can clean paddocks and stalls comfortably. I can trim my horse's feet – though I plan to accept a little help. I am so amazingly blessed to be in the company of horses that my spirit threatens to burst some times. I learn more about relationship and leadership every time I am with one of my horses. I cherish putting my cheek to Bo or Swizzle's soft muzzle to inhale the wonderful scent of *horse*. It is enough. It is a feast.

~

If the small things of relationship aren't enough there will never be anything big enough *to* matter.

Reasons why people fail to find satisfaction and daily blessings include boredom, lack of time, feelings of self-consciousness or embarrassment, or inadequate motivation or attention. No one is impressed when you share a nap under a shady oak tree with your horse. No blue ribbon is awarded for riding bareback through the pasture woods. Cleaning hooves, stalls, paddocks, and tack are chores for some but delights to others.

The old story about the little girl who received a jar of pony manure for Christmas continues to be told because it is simply profound. What would most children think if their parents gave them horse manure as a gift? They might be appalled, insulted, disappointed, or feel abused. Not this little girl. The beribboned jar of pony manure was a promise of what waited outside. She ran to the door in search of the pony! It's a silly story, but anyone who has lived through a serious colic episode looks at manure as wonderful stuff, proof of health and that their horse is well.

The heights of relationship are only achieved when the practical and sometimes repetitive details of life are transformed into gems of promise. Nothing survives in the thin air atop the highest peaks. One may visit, but nothing can actually live there.

The Apostle Paul and Jesus' disciples did not spend their days in transcendent states of bliss walking lofty spiritual heights. The details of their journeys recorded in God's Word showcase a few singular blooms in an otherwise weed-fouled garden of hunger, imprisonment, rejection, and martyrdom. The Garden of Eden remains closed but the gate to heaven was opened by Jesus Christ. New Creations walk the narrow path that will – eventually – lead you there to take up residence in a mansion He has prepared especially for you. [John 14:2-3]

The victory feast of Jesus Christ is consumed one bite at a time. Freedom and the gifts of the Spirit are yours in each moment of your journey. Savor each one.

Three music ministers visited our barn home to enjoy fellowship and meet the horses on a closer and more personal basis. We've known two of the group for years. We first met at a little church in Poolville, Texas where I played the organ for a very forgiving congregation.

The beginning of a years-long friendship began and deepens each time we meet. The title of my second book, *He Came Looking for Me*, was inspired by a song on David Fowler's first solo album. A very personal testimony shared by another member of the group found its way into the pages of that book as further proof of just how true God's promises are and that we are never outside of His care. One of the original group retired and another married. The new trio, Made by Mercy, is made up of two of the three original Davids and the new Mrs. David.

Conversation that afternoon covered an entire road course of topics, from horses to missionary work, high school sports to Christian apologetics. Each of us is well read and founded in both scholarship and personal experience – our guests in particular. During the visit Mrs. David commented about something that "*Enough is as good as a feast.*"

This concept wasn't unfamiliar to me, but the way this short sentence sums it up struck me broadside. It is a simple truth, but sadly foreign to the majority of folks trying to make it through today, this month, and this year in order to get to a "better" place somewhere down the road.

Whenever I share something I didn't come up with myself I like to attribute it appropriately. I had just turned my car toward home after saying goodbye to the Davids and Mrs. David at the motel when I realized I had already forgotten the source of the quote. I quickly executed a U-turn and returned to the lobby to see if I could catch Mrs. David before she went up to her room.

"Who," I asked breathlessly, "was it that said, 'Enough is as good as a feast.' I plan to use it and want to attribute it correctly but I've already forgotten who said it." I was expecting to hear the name of a famous author or minister in answer to my query, "Who said it?"

Mrs. David looked at me with an "interesting" expression and replied, "Mary Poppins."

Not some famous theologian, but a character wrapped up in simple truth nevertheless. I wished everyone good night and said we'd see them in the morning at the church they were visiting.

Christians know that enough *is* the feast. Jesus is "all in all" and "all we'll ever need. " The moment you were born again in Christ your need of *more* ended. There is no addition or increase necessary to deliver salvation and eternal life; Christ paid it all at Calvary. The last word Jesus spoke before He died, "Tetelestai" is translated from the Greek as "It is finished" or "Paid in full." In the context of enough, Jesus declared that no more was needed. It was done.

Animals Know How to Live

Horses don't care about goals. Neither do dogs. Animals are simple. Nature is simple. Horses care about spirit, security, food, rest, play, and companionship. Horses are herd animals hard-wired by their Creator to seek relationship. Dogs care about food, sleep, play, fellowship, and will happily interrupt their travel to investigate an interesting sound or odor. Dogs are pack animals hard-wired by their Creator to seek relationship.

Horses and dogs will literally stop to smell the roses. How else will they know if the blooms are edible or if someone they know passed by recently? Sniffing the environment is like checking the canine version of Facebook. *Who's been here? What did they do? Who did they do it with? Which way did they go?*

Horses and dogs are outstanding power-nappers and often share a soft shady spot with a friend. Horses and dogs are far better at relationships than people. Dogs are beloved for their loyalty. Dogs will remain faithful to an undeserving owner, put up with little kids painfully tugging at ears or tails, and show grace and forgiveness even when it is undeserved.

Horses and dogs know what's important. They aren't conflicted. Horses and dogs don't look at a half full water bucket and fret that half is gone. They look into the bucket of water when thirsty and take a drink. They trust that the necessities of life will be provided.

> *"Therefore do not worry, saying, 'What shall we eat?' or 'What shall we drink?' or 'What shall we wear?' For your heavenly Father knows that you need all these things." – Matthew 6:31-32*

The blessing of relationship is the journey itself, not some imagined or mystical destination. Right relationship is enough, not the pursuit of more. People who don't have enough, who keep pressing on for further gain, don't realize that what they seek is relationship. There is no thing or material item that will ever satisfy the hunger to belong; to love; to find security; to know God.

The measure of true success on your journey of life is determined more by direction than speed. What matters is where you're going and with whom you travel, not how fast you're clicking off the miles.

Enough is as good as a feast.

CHRISTIAN HORSE TRAINING

Christian Horse Training (CHT) is discipleship with horses. CHT concepts are taught using gospel parables, epistles, and behaviors modeled by Christ Himself. There is a world of difference in experience, intent, reward, and promise between devotion to some *one* and devotion to some *thing*.

Relationship with Jesus Christ rests on an immovable foundation of faith, focus, obedience, and transformative relationship; not to any cue, cause, or set of behavioral principles. It is impossible to have a meaningful relationship with a thing; there must be a *somebody* of unique identity who may both know and be known.

Every journey with the Lord is a personal one. CHT focuses on each individual horse and human and not any particular discipline, philosophy, or doctrine of horsemanship. The horses who bless us with relationship haven't read any books on Natural Horsemanship, Classical Dressage, clicker training, or Christian Horse Training. Horses haven't even read the Bible, yet they are not conflicted about the nature and identity of their Creator or the spirit He gave them and the plan by which they live.

At its best, every training method that emphasizes relationship and horse sense over dominance strives to establish communication with a horse in order to earn its trust, obedience and participation in a hybrid of leader-follower and partnership relationship. The words *must, should, always,* and *never* have little use when the subject is relationship.

There are norms as well as exceptions among horses and humans. CHT uses our relationship with horses to mirror the one we have with Jesus Christ – and vice versa. God wastes nothing and I've seen CHT work both ways. It brings a Christian clarity with his or her horse as well as introduces the truth of God's Word to experienced and committed equestrians.

Everything of true value in life must somehow connect to a relationship. Objects, education, and experiences have no intrinsic value that is appreciated by all people, nations, or eras. Gold cannot feed a hungry child. The most highly educated philosopher or theologian may not know how to grow a carrot.

The quality of your life equals the quality of your relationships. Mundane, sordid, and miserable lives can be transformed into extraordinary, inspirational, and victorious ones through relationship. You passed from condemnation into glory when you become a New Creation in Jesus Christ. CHT transforms a horse's nature from prey animal to one of confidence and faith by relationship with a worthy human leader.

The miracle of rebirth in Christ forgives your past, transforms your present, and secures your future. But it isn't the end. Jesus' promise and gift of eternal joy and a peace that passes all understanding are yours for the taking. Rebirth is both a promise and fact that establishes a new beginning; a new journey.

The quality of your life, your faith, and your future rests in the quality of your relationships. If you're investing precious resources of time, energy, and capital on something unrelated to a relationship, what are you investing for?

Horses are unique, because like God they treat us exactly as we deserve unless they show us grace. Horses not only read our body language but our energy and our spirit. Come to a horse relationship with an agenda of "My way or the highway" and you'll have a fight on your hands. Approach a horse with simple love, offer worthy leadership or partnership, and it will respond in spades.

Gospel Messages from the Horse

Horses gift us with their presence and power, their devotion and dedication, their personality and predictability. What life lessons can we learn from horses? Which gospel messages are enacted on the hoof for our enlightenment?

- Personal accountability
- Forgiveness
- Effort - Try
- Patience
- Dedication
- Fellowship - Play
- Perseverance - Hope

Horses offer humans an example of willingness to sacrifice self for the benefit of 'the herd.' What great lessons do horses teach humans? Simplicity, honesty, and the difference between the real world based upon God's design and a virtual world based upon man's design.

Unlike people, horses do not lie to themselves or each other. For a nearly perfect reflection of who you are look deep into the eyes of a horse.

There is as much difference between a Christian horse trainer and Christian Horse Training as there is between a Christian author and Christian writing. The former describes the faith of the human while the latter defines the work itself.

CHT makes promises to horses they can understand. One of those promises is protection. CHT offers worthy leadership to every horse by applying a scriptural foundation and the principles of each trainer's own walk with Jesus Christ. In other words, as Christ is the head of the trainer, so the trainer is the "head" of the horse.

Great horsemen and horsewomen create relationships with horses using the principles of equine herd leadership. To achieve success leaders must understand the equine spirit, patterns of thought, and both recognize and use body language as a method of communication. Horses are born looking for leadership. CHT hopes to enhance and elevate the wonder that is *horse,* not to change it.

Great trainers walk among horses, understand the fears, temptations, and emotions horses experience, and use that wisdom to transform horses from reactionary prey animals into new creations of faith and fearlessness through relationship.

God sent Jesus to us for that same purpose. Jesus walked among us and personally experienced human fears, human temptations, and human emotions. No one will ever experience the limit of what is possible through right relationship with Jesus Christ. No one will ever achieve the limit of what is possible in a life well-lived with horses. The blessing is in the journey itself.

The following simple bullet-point lists spell out the complete CHT formula for successfully training horses. If you are already a master of these rules and perform them perfectly every day, you don't need to read any further. But if you can't (and truthfully, no one can) the remainder of this book explains, illustrates, and highlights the difficulties and pitfalls such basic concepts present to complex humans, and some simple (but not necessarily easy) techniques to apply them.

The challenge for most of us is getting past our experience and education to be simple enough to execute these few rules well. Tradition, habits, and history create serious stumbling blocks on the path to transformative relationship with God and horses.

This outline covers every issue in horse training from basic ground manners to Grand Prix or other elite level of competition. The level you achieve depends entirely on your commitment and skill in applying these simple rules.

Foundational Requirements for Relationship:

- Show Up
- Focus
- Offer Obedience

CHT Basic commands:

- Come
- Follow
- Go
- Yield

Steps to Leadership Success:

- Ask a simple yes/no question. PRECISELY verbalize/define the correct answer before asking.
- Did the horse answer yes or no?
- If yes, QUIT asking.
- If no, Why? – Is the horse Unable or Unwilling?
- Respond appropriately: Make able, Motivate, or Move on.

Most of you will run into a few snags when you apply these rules. Any time your horse becomes anxious, aggressive, or angry you failed. Little snags quickly become bigger problems once discouragement and frustration get into the act. If problems get too big most folks are tempted to quit. But don't give up. The purpose of CHT is to solve problems by building faith.

Everyone wins.

UNABLE OR UNWILLING

Failure is always due to (1) inability or (2) unwillingness. Success is elusive when someone is UNABLE to do as needed or someone is UNWILLING to do what is needed. Usually that 'someone' is the person looking back at you in the bathroom mirror each morning. Are there exceptions? Sure. But that just means that someone else who mattered to the success of your plans or goals was either unable or unwilling to do as required.

Do either of these sound familiar?

"I can't!"

"I won't!"

These are the most basic forms of expressing inability and unwillingness. Henry Ward Beecher summed it up pretty well when he said, *"The difference between perseverance and obstinacy is that one comes from a strong will and the other from a strong won't."*

Seldom is anything that easy when you're talking about grown up folks or even little humans over the age of five. Has one of your kids ever tried to disguise a strong WON'T with a pitiful little whine, "But I can't"? Ask yourself, *have*

*I ever tried to get out of something by saying 'I can't'
rather than 'I won't'?* Be honest, no one else is listening
and this little conversation is just between you and me.

Of course you have! When the nice lady from church asked
you to work on that committee or your spouse asked you to
do one of your least favorite projects - have you NEVER
offered an excuse for why you *can't* do as asked when in
reality you just *didn't want to*?

"Sorry, but I just don't have time" translates to *"I don't
want to."* People always find time for the things they really
want to do.

Most Christian Horse Training events begin with a
challenge. Horses that do not do as owners ask are usually
deemed unwilling by both the handler and much of the
audience. The truth in most instances is the horses are
unable to obey. It is human nature to begin placing blame
on the other, and not on self.

Failure to develop a transformative relationship with Jesus
Christ is always our fault. He cannot send His Spirit into a
human heart closed to everything but self-interest.

Focusing on self above all else results in:

- Self-justification
- Self-righteousness
- Self-vindication
- Self-satisfaction
- Self-aggrandizement
- Self-preservation
- Self-satisfaction

- Self-centeredness
- Self-doubt
- Self-loathing

God cannot enter, much less use, an unbroken heart. Who looks for a solution unless she has a problem? Who seeks enlightenment until he realizes he is in darkness? Who seeks a physician until she realizes she is ill? Who seeks a Savior unless he realizes he needs one?

Until one recognizes that rationalization, excuse, and self-idolatry cannot solve many problems or needs, and that nothing we can or know how to do has the power to transform the present, there is no desire to listen, learn, accept, repent, or seek a solution apart from one's own strength or power. People who are supremely self-confident in their own power to provide, resolve, and order the universe to their liking have eyes only on the face in the mirror. Once they admit their inability to solve the problem or fill the need they become able to look elsewhere.

Changing one's focus from the face in the mirror to the face of God creates a beginning. Until there is a need, why seek a solution? Once a need is recognized one must be willing to learn, practice, submit, and focus. God will never ask you to do something you are unable to do, but He will never MAKE you accept His will and power.

You cannot establish the beginning of relationship with a horse that refuses to acknowledge your presence. You cannot establish transformative relationship with a horse unless it is willing to focus on you - and you are willing to focus on the horse.

God never makes a request or sends anyone out to do something he or she is unable to accomplish. There is nothing God will ask you to do without providing the means. Our part is to show up, focus, and be willing.

When did you get off track?

One day it hits you, "I'm not the success I thought I would be. My career isn't stellar; my marriage is far from perfect, my kids think I'm irrelevant and lately even my horse pins her ears when I feed her. Even my faith is as limp as overcooked spaghetti." The next thought is usually, "How did I get here? When did I get off the right track?" And then, "What can I do to fix my life?"

Each one of these failed or underperforming parts of your life is off-track for one of two reasons - and the same two reasons apply to all of them, from your cranky pony to your relationship with God. In each instance someone is either unwilling to do what he should or is unable to do what is needed.

It isn't always possible to achieve multiple goals the way you hope or plan. When you realize that the actual facts of your circumstances reveal conflicting goals, you must choose which one is most important because you cannot walk two roads or live two different lives at the same time.

One fact needs to be perfectly clear - no one is responsible for the state of your career, marriage, relationship with your children, your horse, or your faith except you. Popular culture pushes the enticing drug of victimhood, encouraging you to lay blame at the feet of that elusive *someone else* who should have prevented you from making wrong decisions. Don't buy what they're selling. You got yourself here, and the only way out is on a trail you must blaze.

If you're not going in the direction you intended to go, STOP. Before you take another step, speak another word, or invest another dollar, take stock of where you are today. If you're not on the road you intended, you must determine exactly where you are NOW so you can figure out which direction you need to go before taking your next step. It's a sure bet that doing the same thing tomorrow you did today will only take you further down the wrong road and make the journey back just that much longer.

Addressing Unwillingness

The number one cure for unwillingness is motivation. Necessity is the mother of invention because need is a great motivator. You get motivated to act when failing to act creates a burden greater than you can bear. In other words, motivation is sufficient when the benefit outweighs the effort or the penalty of failure is greater than the effort required.

How long would you keep working to accomplish a particular goal if previous experience proved it was impossible? Why tilt with a windmill that beats you every time? What happens to motivation when expectations are so high that no level of achievement will ever be enough?

Lots of folks still smoke cigarettes. Do they smoke because they don't know that it's bad? No. They smoke because they want to. It's a form of Russian Roulette. Their choice – their responsibility.

Why are there so many unwanted pregnancies in the United States? Is it because the parties involved don't know how babies are made? No. They want to do what they want to do. They are unwilling to prevent pregnancy, not unable. They're just playing the odds.

Isn't it odd how people are willing to play the odds with God? The only reason someone isn't focused on, and obedient to, God's Word is because he or she can't or won't. The same is true of horses.

Two rules generally apply when you're not sure whether your problem stems from unwillingness or inability.

Rule #1 - Grace

When you're not sure whether someone is unable or unwilling, the first rule requires you to give him the benefit of your doubt. This is an example of grace.

Pretend you asked your daughter before she left for school this morning to pick up the envelope on the kitchen table containing a permission slip for a special event and take it to her teacher. A half hour later you buzz through the kitchen and see the envelope still lying on the table. What's your first thought?

"Teenagers, you can't trust them to do even the smallest thing."

I bet the first thing that occurred to you wasn't how to get the envelope to its destination- or to wait until you ask your daughter about it before making any assumption about why she didn't take the envelope to school. If it was, you may already be a master of building great relationships and I tip my hat to you.

The usual response when someone doesn't do as you ask is to assume he or she (a) chose not to do it on purpose, (b) has a less than stellar character, or (c) was absent the day smarts were handed out.

People do the same thing with their horses. Why isn't your horse consistent? Why isn't he obedient? Why did he perform so well yesterday but screw up today? Did he (a) fail on purpose, (b) exhibit his negative personality, or (c) prove that he's simply not very bright?

Judging someone's motives by guesswork alone is normal, human, and expected - but is a bad habit and unbecoming a Christian (Matthew 7:1-5, Romans 2:17-20).

Maybe your daughter didn't hear you. Would that bit of information make a difference? It should. Not only was your daughter unable to do as you asked (she can't read your mind) but it makes the fault for the failure 100% yours. How many times have you asked a family member or co-worker to do something when you couldn't see them or didn't know if they actually heard what you said?

When your horse disappoints you is he able to do as you ask but unwillingly to obey? Are you sure he understood what you asked? Responsible horse owners rule out physical issues first when a horse refuses to do what is asked. Some mornings I wake up with a hitch in my getalong for no good reason at all. Some days you're the windshield and some days you're the bug. Horses have bug days too. Discerning the truth of the situation is your responsibility.

Pitfalls of Making Assumptions

Imagine you're walking down the street with a friend when a very heavy woman passes by on the other side. Your friend says, "Why doesn't that woman do something about her weight? What could she be thinking to be that fat?"

There's a distinct possibility you've had a similar thought yourself. Many people practice instant judgment and say or do things that reflect more poorly on them than the object of the derisive comment. Some people aren't even as polite as your friend.

What *one more fact* might there be in this lady's case? Since I'm making this up anyway, let's pretend you actually know the lady on the other side of the street. After your friend's remark you politely reply, "That's Andrea. I know her from church. Do you realize that she's already lost 150 pounds in the past year? She is such an inspiration."

Gulp.

Maybe you know someone who used to be a very successful barrel racer. She rode anything and did it well. But last week you saw her just walking and jogging around on one of her experienced horses and got off balance when the horse bumped into a canter for a few strides.

Wow, she's not as good as I thought she was. I ride better than she does!

What you don't know is that the barrel racer had a stroke. Facts change and so do people and horses. There is always a degree of assumption and probability that we're wrong when we judge anything from our present knowledge and perspective alone. Would you want others to judge you without all the facts about your situation?

> *"For in the same way you judge others, you will be judged, and with the measure you use, it will be measured to you."* – Matthew 7:2

We're not machines and neither are horses. Have you ever simply been off with no particular reason? Some days you're the windshield and some days you're the bug. If your horse is having a bug day, respond with hands of mercy.

When in doubt, give grace.

Rule #2 - Take smaller steps

When you don't know whether the problem is one of unwillingness or inability there is a second rule to apply. When you can't determine if someone is unable or unwilling apply Rule #1 and offer grace – even when the one in question is you. *That's all well and good*, you say, *but what is the next practical step*?

The next step is to stop the cycle of failure and begin to create a little success. The way you build the habit and history of success is to break down the project, problem, lesson, or maneuver into smaller steps and consistently conquer the tiniest baby steps; one at a time.

Mathematicians recognize that between any two points there is always another point, and another point between any two of the now three points, and so on into infinity. The same is true when moving toward a goal. Between any two steps there is always a smaller step.

When things go wrong the trick is to figure out the precise point where the trouble first appeared. The only way to address the actual cause of failure or detour is to identify the moment your plan took a wrong turn and address the problem at its source. If you make one wrong turn, then another, then another, you won't get back on track if you only look at your most recent mistake. At best that simply puts you in a different wrong place.

What happened before the horse bucked?

A lady who was bucked off her horse on a recent trail ride asked me what she could possibly have done differently to avoid hitting the ground. After asking a series of questions I discovered her horse began to behave in a nervous and anxious manner twenty minutes before he bucked.

The problem wasn't a bucking horse, but whatever caused the horse to become anxious and nervous in the first place. The lady received a twenty minute window of grace from her horse but didn't recognize the opportunity to step up and handle the horse's problem. She just kept riding, getting more frustrated and nervous just as her horse's anxiety continued to grow.

The time to act is the instant you recognize a "No." Usually the first *I can't* or *I won't* is presented softly or hesitantly. Horses and humans rarely offer hooves, heels, or fists as the first sign of resistance. Seldom is the first "no" delivered verbally, but visually by a change in posture or expression.

You'll never figure out why the chicken crossed the road if the first time you thought about it the chicken was already on the other side and moving on. What was the chicken doing when it came to the road? It had to choose to stay on one side or cross the dangerous byway. What was the decision process? Was there a wily coyote on its little chicken heels or was a there a truly lovely Miss Chicken on the other side? Maybe the chicken started the day on the other side and was just going home.

Don't make assumptions after the fact. Begin to fix a problem the instant you recognize you have one otherwise you'll be working on the wrong problem.

The Power to Chose

Recognizing that you always have the power to choose is as important as properly identifying all available options. You may find yourself at a crossroad or detour you never wanted to see, but the power to choose which direction to move is yours.

Discrimination, victimhood, and those nasty negative bits of self-talk that plague everyone sooner or later try to convince you that you have no power, no options, and no opportunity. All are effective lies the Enemy uses to trick you into quitting. He got the best of Adam and Eve, so don't think that you are not in his evil crosshairs as well.

Christians are never victims, and if you are reading this you're still in the world (John 17:15, 2 Corinthians 5:15). Where did God's Word ever tell you that you have no power, no options, no opportunity, and no value? Where is the message of victimhood found in the Bible? It's not there! What God's Word does say is that you are more than a conqueror (Romans 8:37).

No one took your opportunity from you. No one prevented you from merging onto the road leading to success. No one robbed you of an important relationship. You get to choose what you do or don't do and how you feel about it.

> *"Everything can be taken from a man but one thing: the last of human freedoms - to choose one's attitude in any given set of circumstances, to choose one's own way."* – Viktor E. Frankl, Holocaust survivor

Choosing is often the biggest gripe we have because we don't want to choose one thing OR the other; we want BOTH. The simplest choice for Christians is between God and Not God; Jesus Christ or not. When you chose Christ you gained entrance to the path leading to the narrow gate of Matthew 7 and left the broad boulevard of the worldly.

Anyone who tells you that it is possible to "have it all" is an idiot or has an ulterior motive. You can't be single and married. You can't be a vegetarian and a consumer of all things hamburger. You can't be primarily focused on your career if you are primarily focused on your family. You can't spend the weekend playing with the kids and slave over a hot computer at the office. You can't live in a virtual world and the real world.

You can pursue transformative relationship with your horse or something less. The moment any goal becomes more important than the promises made to your horse, you choose the road leading to another goal. Transformative relationship is everything or nothing.

You can't serve two masters. This is such a simple truth. But how many people consider it when making plans for their lives? You can't run with the devil all day and come home to the Lord's house in the evening. You can't walk with God and the world at the same time. You can't celebrate the birth of one grandchild while celebrating the freedom of your daughter to abort another.

You can fool yourself but you can't fool God.

At the corner of Unable and Unwilling

A main component of introduction to CHT is the discussion of the two causes of all failure and learning how to distinguish which plagues you at the moment, inability or unwillingness.

The fork in the road leading to Unwillingness may be a dead end, but the fork in the road of Inability has many potential destinations. But if you really DON'T WANT to make a change then you are choosing more of the same over something different and potentially far better. Don't blame anyone else, this is your choice.

Leadership and self-awareness are not fully-developed gifts you can unwrap and put to immediate use. Once you know which challenge you face, inability or unwillingness, you have to figure out what to do to fix it.

Enforcement, or punishment, will never fix inability—and no amount of education will ever fix unwillingness.

There are three basic options to address "I can't" and "I won't":

1. Make able.

2. Motivate, or

3. Move on.

~

This is a good place to share a word about wisdom. Who doesn't want to be wise? Doesn't wisdom bring success? I've thought about wisdom a lot lately.

To paraphrase Solomon, wisdom is never granted. Wisdom is earned or achieved through common sense perseverance. Wisdom is the result of first being broken and then repaired. Wisdom means you learn not to repeat the same mistake a second time. Wisdom is highly sought after because so few seem to ever find it.

"Experience is not what happens to you; it's what you do with what happens to you." - Aldous Huxley

MASTERSHIP AND OBEDIENCE

"To have a master and teacher is not the same thing as being mastered and taught. Having a master and teacher means that there is someone who knows me better than I know myself, who is closer than a friend, and who understands the remotest depths of my heart and is able to satisfy them fully. It means having someone who has made me secure in the knowledge that he has met and solved all the doubts, uncertainties, and problems in my mind. To have a master and teacher is this and nothing less—
Our Lord never takes measures to make me do what He wants. Sometimes I wish God would master and control me to make me do what He wants, but He will not. And at other times I wish He would leave me alone, and He does not." - Oswald Chambers

CHT offers worthy leadership to a horse that is similar to the mastership Jesus Christ offers His chosen ones. Some horse folks think that mastership is by definition punitive and unfair. Saint Francis of Assisi regularly appealed to God on behalf of man and beast. Referring to animals Francis wrote, *"Not to hurt our humble brethren is our first duty to them, but to stop there is not enough. We have a higher mission -- to be of service to them wherever they require it."*

Did God deliver up the beautiful creatures of His creation to man as servants, as chattel, as soulless resources for future carnivores? When God gave man dominion over animals did that imply that humans are of inestimable value and animals of very little; that they walk and swim about aimlessly unless selected to serve or be sacrificed for man?

If that were true how could man and beast share transformative relationship? Once you experience any life-changing relationship with another person, horse, dog, or other creature you know how it made your world bigger, richer, and fundamentally changed you. People that have never experienced such magic have a far greater mountain to climb in the pursuit of faith that drives out fear because the only path to salvation for man is transformational relationship with Jesus Christ.

CHT uses the principles of worthy leadership to transform horses from prey animal to partner. Fear is the predominant driver of equine behavior. It is fear that motivates the feet to head for the hills without thinking twice. Horses bolt from fear. Bucking and rearing aren't the result of strength in action, but of anger, anxiety, or aggression - obvious signs that the horse has a problem.

Fear is also the driving force behind a great deal of human behavior. Horses experience fear as prey animals. Faith in a worthy leader eliminates most fear from horses once experience proves that the human who controls their feet, guarantees their safety, understands their needs and perplexities, will – in every situation – protect them from danger.

Faith in Jesus Christ, the most worthy leader, removes fear from the hearts of Christians. Faith grows as the process of spiritual relationship proceeds and experience teaches us that Christ is in control of everything, He guarantees our present peace and ultimate safety, understands every need and perplexity, and will – in every circumstance – protect us from the evil one until the day we move into our heavenly mansion. [John 14:2]

CHT also uses the experience and truth of life lived with horses to introduce Jesus Christ to non-Christians. Trainers who have never seriously considered the gospel message are stunned when they discover that the promises, authority, dedication, sacrifice, passion, forgiveness, childlike simplicity, and foundations of leading a horse to faith are all written in God's Word.

Horses crave attention and access to beloved masters. Christians do the same. The power of faith to eliminate fear is found in this simple story:

Seeing the Master

*A sick man turned to his doctor as he was preparing to
Leave the examination room and said,
'Doctor, I am afraid to die.
Tell me what lies on the other side.'
Very quietly, the doctor said, 'I don't know.'
'You don't know? You, a Christian man,
Do not know what is on the other side?'
The doctor was holding the handle of the door;
On the other side came a sound of scratching and
whining,
And as he opened the door, a dog sprang into the room*

And leaped on him with an eager show of gladness.
Turning to the patient, the doctor said,
'Did you notice my dog?
He's never been in this room before.
He didn't know what was inside.
He knew nothing except that his master was here,
And when the door opened, he sprang in without fear.
I know little of what is on the other side of death,
But I do know one thing...
I know my Master is there and that is enough.'
- author unknown

Access to the throne of God isn't our right. It is a promise of Jesus Christ to His children that we will one day be permitted entrance into His presence. No power on earth can grant an audience with the King of Kings except that bestowed by the Holy Spirit through rebirth as a New Creation.

There is another message being preached that has been twisted into a lie. Too many people hear a permissive parenting message of entitlement in the words, "Jesus loves me, this I know, for the Bible tells me so." God so loved us that He sent His Son to die that we might be saved and live in eternity in His presence, but Calvary is not a *Get Out of Jail Free* card for those who refuse to allocute, to admit their guilt. Jesus Christ isn't just your Savior; He is your Lord and Master (John 13:13).

How popular do you think the idea of accepting a master is in the 21st century? The world's growing interest in the religion of self-actualization preaches the polar opposite of having any master aside from one's own interests. In many intellectual, social, and religious camps the Mount Everest of human growth today is complete self-awareness and self-absorption. You can sum up the doctrine of progressive culture from the 1960's as "If it feels good, do it," which leaves absolutely no room or tolerance for a master.

Abraham Maslow, famous for his *Hierarchy of Needs* studied by every student of psychology, characterized self-actualizers as people who accept their own human nature with all its flaws and view the shortcomings of others and the contradictions of the human condition with humor and tolerance. Sadly, Mr. Maslow failed to consider God's opinion. No one would need a Savior if God tolerated sin with humor.

Christians are not immune from self-importance and presumption, especially when it comes to Christ. Most Christians would not dream of visiting Buckingham Palace in London with the expectation of knocking on the Queen's door to gain entrance as an equal, yet think of Jesus and access to the very throne of God as their right. Some denominations preach that there is no requirement at all to receive full rights, privileges, and benefits of heaven. People don't even have to believe in or like Jesus. They're in just because they're human.

How could anyone think more about correct behavior, demeanor, appropriate reverence, and being properly submissive to royal protocol before an earthly monarch than the God who created the Universe? Than with the Christ who died that they might live?

The lack of respect for God is the basic reason some present-day Christians harbor fear and insecurity and make such poor leaders for horse or human. The God revealed in Psalm 97 and Isaiah 45 is not reverenced because His power is presumed as a right of adoption, but because He is God. The Israelites errantly believed they were entitled to God's blessing and provision because He owed it to them. Has this same sense of entitlement really changed?

> *"For thus says the* LORD, *Who created the heavens, Who is God, Who formed the earth and made it, Who has established it, Who did not create it in vain, Who formed it to be inhabited: "I am the* LORD, *and there is no other." – Isaiah 45:18*

Jesus as Master

Jesus as Master provides all you need and will equip you to do everything He asks yet will never force you to obey. Have you ever prayed, "Lord, would you just make me obedient?" Have you every prayed, "Lord, would you just leave me alone?" Such prayers are 100% me-centered.

Focusing on our own desires, 'I, Me, Mine," removes our focus from where it can have any power. Our attention leaves the throne and majesty of God when we settle it on ourselves. Frantic or confused horses often become manageable when blindfolded because their focus is restricted to the handler, and not on their own opinion of what's happening around them.

The new message shouted from the roof tops, the seats of political power, the ivory towers of education, and many pulpits is one of tolerance and equality. Having a master has become synonymous with slavery.

New Creations in Christ pray for God to:

- Teach them
- Train them
- Mold them
- Equip them
- Correct them
- Perfect them
- Inspire them …

… so that they may be useful to Him, bring glory to Him, and continually seek His vision and His truth. All that is good is from Him. Your future rests in Him.

Horses and Masters

One definition of master describes an individual *eminently skilled* in something, like a Master Gardener. Jesus Christ is eminently skilled in everything that is, was, or will be. He is Master – especially of relationships.

Being mastered usually means one must serve as directed or be punished. Being mastered is the state of being under the authority, whim, power, or disposition of the one who is able to maintain the position as master. Having a master is associated today more with hatred, slavery, and intolerance than with security.

Political correctness has merged what are actually two separate circumstances into one – one of authoritative domination that denies the existence of a Master who cares, loves, and preserves – a Master who gave His own life for those who call Him "Lord." Such a Master does exist – Jesus.

Secure in Christ, you reap the blessings and rewards of being a sheep in His flock. Do you wish to leave the care of the Good Shepherd or are you content and dedicated to remain as close to Him as possible day by day and moment by moment? It is Jesus Christ who leads you beside the still waters, restores your soul, and brings you to verdant green pastures for provision and rest. How well do you think you would fare as a sheep on your own?

Is it right that horses should have a master? There is a difference in opinion in the equine world about that question. Is it fair to require a horse to respect your personal space when you are not required to respect his? Is it fair to burden a horse with saddle, bridle, and rider? Is it fair to ask a horse to earn its living by serving the one who provides room and board?

Is it right that you should aspire to be your horse's leader in the first place? Is that demeaning or destructive? One equine-related school of thought acknowledges no definition of leadership or master that is not domineering and coercive.

These simple comparisons may help you process the difference between leadership and dominance:

- God leads. Satan pushes.
- God offers. God provides. Satan tempts. Satan confiscates.
- God seeks to perfect. Satan seeks to corrupt.
- God seeks relationship. Satan seeks to isolate you from God.

- God makes decisions about things beyond your understanding to protect you and your interests. Satan seeks your destruction.
- God is truth. Satan is a liar.

Transformative relationship with Jesus Christ is built on faith that builds hope, perseverance, and leads to glory. The process of sanctification builds confidence and not fear. Like Paul, I hope you are persuaded that nothing can come between the Master and you (Romans 8:28).

> *"Therefore, having been justified by faith, ... we have access by faith into this grace in which we stand, and rejoice in hope of the glory of God. And not only that, but we also glory in tribulations, knowing that tribulation produces perseverance; and perseverance, character; and character, hope. Now hope does not disappoint, because the love of God has been poured out in our hearts by the Holy Spirit who was given to us." – Romans 5:1-5*

Coercion promotes fear. The only faith coercion builds is faith that every additional interaction will also have a negative result. CHT reveals dominance as a house built on sand and washes it away to reveal the rock solid eternal foundation of faith in Christ.

Offering to be a devoted master to your horse is both a blessing and a responsibility. It is a commitment, a promise, and journey of transformative relationship. Some people believe Christians delude themselves into accepting the dominant authority of a nasty deity. They have never met Jesus Christ. Some people believe it isn't possible to offer a horse something *more* by worthy leadership and that those who think they can are also kidding themselves.

Accepting the role of master to a horse – a worthy leader – places the burden of success firmly on the shoulders of the human. Errors are the fault of the person. Failure is always human failure. To be a master is to offer; to provide; to seek to perfect; to seek transformative relationship. It requires making decisions beyond the understanding of the horse to both protect it and its interests.

It is not possible for a human to be the perfect leader or master to a horse. Proper authority is always balanced with humility. Horses show us exactly where we need to improve. Even when we make a mistake they forgive. How noble. Lessons aren't only for our horses – there is also a corresponding lesson for us. CHT is discipleship with horses, not horse training.

Jesus Christ is my Master. The longer my journey with Him the better able I am to be a worthy leader and loving master to my horses. There is no way I can truly appreciate the depth of commitment Jesus made to me. But I understand it a bit more each time I stand on the commitment I make to my horses that recognizes no deal breakers, has no expiration date, and contains no fine print.

LEADERSHIP CHARACTERISTICS

Authority is recognized, not proclaimed. One is considered to be authentic when words and actions match, when emotions are genuine, and when he is proven trustworthy and reliable. A worthy leader is authentic. Every promise of a worthy leader is as good as delivered the moment it is spoken. Authority is the result of experience, not rhetoric.

> *"And they were astonished at His teaching, for He taught them as one having authority, and not as the scribes. Then they were all amazed, so that they questioned among themselves, saying, 'What is this? What new doctrine is this? For with authority He commands even the unclean spirits, and they obey Him.'" – Mark 1:22, 27*

Christian Horse Training (CHT) can teach someone skills, but it cannot change character where a resistance to change exists. CHT cannot give anyone the mantle of authority, but its principles and precepts may help you earn it by opening your heart, mind, and spirit to both the humility and authority of Jesus Christ, and demonstrating how that same balance leads to success with your horse (family, students, employees, or congregations.)

Authenticity

"If you say you are sanctified, show it." – Oswald Chambers 8.27

Jesus Christ is God, Spirit, and Savior. He created everything, established the rules, and lived a perfect human life. No other man will ever walk the walk as He did. The most powerful messages are not those delivered by oratory or edict, but by people whose behavior and life is their witness and testimony.

What is your testimony? If a silent movie were made of your life would viewers receive the message you intend? Authenticity is the perfect union of message and action. Authentic leaders are predictable. Each day adds to the weight of their message and example. The more you get to know them the more credible, trustworthy, and pure they become.

Authentic leaders have willing followers and are known for delivering on every single promise made. If you examine the habits of worthy leaders you will note that they never take a coffee break from responsibility and always work with vision and purpose.

Leaders deserving of faith have purposeful plans and an unlimited commitment to help those who follow increase their own levels of confidence and ability. Required sacrifices are not charged as debt to students, disciples, trainees, or horses, but made willingly by the leader.

Ten Traits of Authentic Leaders

Authentic leaders:

1. Know the difference between having a reason based upon fact and excuses intended to evade or limit their liability.

2. Are accountable, accepting the burden of duty. They never rationalize, dodge responsibility, or justify failures.

3. Speak in positive terms of what can be done rather than focusing on what can't be done.

4. Always have a back-up plan and are prepared for contingencies; they do not rely on chance, blaming whatever goes wrong on simple happenstance or outside the limits of their control.

5. Work with vision and purpose; they are not erratic, unstable or unpredictable.

6. Are proactive, controlling events; they are not reactive, letting events control them.

7. Bloom in challenging times; they don't wilt under pressure.

8. Are adaptable and flexible; they are not intractable, nor do they freeze up when confronted with unexpected changes in conditions or plans.

9. Build others up; they do not tear others down.

10. Expect complete integrity and dedication to mission,

personally setting the performance bar; they do not exempt themselves from the same standards asked of others.

Excuses

> *"If I had not come and spoken to them, they would have no sin, but now they have no excuse for their sin." – John 15:22*

The words "but" or "because" often precede a statement of excuse or unwillingness to be responsible, or a lack of conviction and commitment. There are only two reasons you fail to achieve what you intend; inability or unwillingness. Do any of these excuses sound familiar?

"What I did isn't *really* wrong *because* ----"

"I want the same kind of relationship with my horse you have with your horse, *but* ----"

"I am a totally committed and invested parent, *but* my children have been a bit of a disappointment *because* ----"

"I know I shouldn't work my horse until his feet are trimmed, *but* ---"

"I know I said I'd be there, *but* ----"

"I love Jesus more than anything else *but* I don't have time to read the Bible *because* ----"

"I know I pull way too hard on my horse's mouth, *but* ---"

"I would love to study more about living as a New Creation *but* ----"

"Let me know when you offer a Christian Horse Training clinic again. It's so important to me to be the leader my horse needs, *but* I just can't think about that right now *because* ---"

> *"But they all with one accord began to make excuses."*
> *– Luke 14:18*

Jesus never offered one excuse or referred His followers to the fine print on any contract. His Word is true and there has never been or will ever be a greater model of commitment and conviction. His commitment led Him to Calvary.

The currency of leadership is trust - faith in the master's constancy and commitment. The power of habits, common sense, and fear disappear in the soft voice that says, "Follow me." Christians are saved by faith. The power of transformative relationship is also rooted in faith.

The ultimate test of a horse's faith in its master is reflexive, spontaneous obedience in the face of obvious danger. Desensitization is a tool horse trainers use to develop a vocabulary and teach horses how to learn. There is no safety in desensitization. Security is found in relationship.

Horses trapped in burning barns escape when the voice of their master says, "Follow me." Horses that have been desensitized to the controlled flames of a jump circle or obstacle course may learn to ignore the heat and crackling sound. But what might happen to that horse in a blazing barn?

The difference between life and death depends on

relationship not desensitization. Do not confuse knowing what is in the Bible with knowing the one and only subject of the Bible – Jesus Christ.

Common Sense

Common sense is not sense that is common to all, but having good sense about common things.

"It is the obvious which is so difficult to see most of the time. People say 'It's as plain as the nose on your face.' But how much of the nose on your face can you see, unless someone holds a mirror up to you?" - Isaac Asimov

Whether a discussion centers on Christian faith or horse training, excessive education often snuffs out common sense. It is possible to know too much to recognize what is staring you in the face. There is a difference between knowing something and the ability to practically apply that knowledge. Given a choice between the two it is better to know that throwing a rock off a building could injure the person standing below than to simply know about the existence of gravity. Little kids know that what goes up will come down yet have no clue that there is a word for it.

Little kids enjoy more intimate and amazing relationships with horses than most grown-ups. The older you get the less you *observe*. Children communicate with each other; they both listen and speak, observe and are observed. Their intentions are simpler and often more effective. How many six year olds have a problem figuring out if their little six year old friend just said yes or no to a question? Childhood inquiries are simple and direct and so are the answers.

*"Simplicity is the secret of seeing things clearly." –
Oswald Chambers*

One of my favorite true kid/horse stories is about a little
girl who packed a sack lunch and took her horse out for the
day with a friend and her own pony. The two girls decided
to ride up a steep trail to the top of a butte. Neither had
been up to the top before but the trail was distinct so they
set out, one riding the full-size horse and the other a pony.

The girl was about ten years old. Her saddle horse also
served as dad's plow horse but only kids could safely ride
him. When the little girl wanted to ride she went out to the
pasture, pushed on her horse's neck until he dropped it so
she could throw a leg over. The horse then lifted up his
head and neck to settle her onto his back.

On this particular ride the girls had bridles and saddles. The
closer they got to the top of the hill the narrower the trail
became until it was barely wide enough for one horse.
Turning a corner the little girl noticed a fallen tree blocking
the path. There was no way to turn around so the little girl
dismounted, crawled under the lowest branch, then turned
to her horse, pulled on the reins a bit and said, "Come,
Dickie."

Dickie got down on his knees and crawled under the branch
to get to the other side. Once the foursome made it to the
top they found an easier way down.

Would your horse crawl under a tree for you? The little girl
made it clear to Dickie that she expected him to follow her.
Would an adult have even considered asking a horse to do

something so impossible? But the little girl didn't know it was impossible and the day passed without incident.

Kids ask horses simple questions and usually understand the horse's simple response. Horses respond to the energy, body language, and purity of children. The more adults learn about *proper* riding the less they rely on their powers of observation and the greater they fear unpredictable outcomes.

- Is your horse anxious or fearful? Observe his behavior.

- Is your horse aggressive or pushy? Observe his behavior.

- Is your horse angry or upset? Observe his behavior.

Common sense tells you that the horse is not happy about its present circumstances. Common sense tells you to change something and observe the result. Changing something does not mean a bigger bit or longer whip. Think more like a kid. It is the key to the kingdom of heaven as well as a deeper relationship with your horse.

Next time you're in the barn sit on a bale of hay for a spell and consider these questions:

1. Will your horse follow you out of a burning barn?

2. Would your horse crawl under a tree because you expected him to?

Jesus said we must become as little children. Amen.

Discernment

Good intentions married to bad application often leave a path of destruction every bit as devastating as intentional bad acts. Ignorance is not bliss. No one knows what they don't know. But, once you recognize a conflict you become accountable for whatever happens next.

Competing pressures plague every life when the desire to achieve a specific goal is pitted against the pursuit of great relationship. The worst possible outcome is burning a bridge without recognizing it until after the fact when the opportunity to choose is gone.

"I didn't realize what I was doing" may be true, but it won't fix what is already broken. Wise people take steps to avoid making the same mistake a second time. Mistakes are going to happen, but let's at least be creative enough to invent new ones and not revisit old ones. Making the same mistake a second time may indicate that it wasn't really a mistake at all, but a choice you made and are simply trying to put a good face on it.

The potential for relationship destruction appears in every aspect of life; with families, friends, co-workers, horses and pets, and most importantly, with God Himself. If you register the emotions of anger, aggression, or anxiety in yourself or others, it's time to examine your situation before lighting a torch.

~

Since my knee was replaced I've worked to eliminate bad habits formed during the years I compensated for a useless right leg. I rode a couple of times with a dressage trainer whose eagle eye caught every error. Her coaching was vital as I prepared to return to active riding.

Early in my rehabilitation process I was given an arena exercise to perform with Bo, one of my amazing grays. At the end of my attempt to perform it properly I KNEW there was something wrong. I was over-cueing Bo with both hands and legs and not getting the result I wanted.

Since 99.99% of every problem with a horse is the fault of the human involved I had no doubt where the blame lay. Where had I gone wrong and what did I need to do to fix myself and offer Bo better leadership?

Nothing in life is more important to me than maintaining right relationship with God, my horses, and with other folks who are so very precious to me. Bo is close to the very top of my list of important relationships. I also like to set goals. Sometimes two good goals conflict. The trick is recognizing the conflict before a skirmish becomes a war.

I had several working goals when I met the riding coach. First, I needed objective eyes to help me correct my body and balance. Next, I wanted to learn more about classical dressage.

Two highly qualified dressage trainers worked out of my training facility for several years. While there are similarities, real differences exist between training a dressage horse and a stock horse - whether you ride western or English.

For me, the greatest difference involves bridle skills.

Dressage riders teach horses to seek significant contact with the bit while I have always promised my horses that there is a place of perfect peace with absolutely no pressure on rein or bit when they are correct. Dressage sees perfection as constant light bit contact intended to support or balance. Perfection to me has always been no bit contact at all.

Bo believes that pressure on rein or bit means he is doing something wrong. It's frustrating to try your best but never get it right. Such experience usually kills the motivation that produces willingness. The past couple of years for Bo and me were mostly messing around bareback since I couldn't school one side of his body.

Not only did the problematic exercise require Bo to be on the bit, but to extend, collect, and perform power moves he had never been taught. I was throwing months worth of new stuff at him in one lesson.

I asked Bo to do the exercise longer than I should have. No damage done, but I realized I was at the crossroads between pleasing my coach and being a worthy leader to Bo. I couldn't do both.

When I got home I decided to break down the whole exercise into all of its parts. You can only teach a horse one new thing at a time. Foundational skills can be combined in endless variations, but those skills have to be in place before you can call upon them. Doing otherwise sets your horse up for frustration, anxiety, or retaliation.

It's possible for horses to learn to distinguish between

styles of riding. My first real show horse knew that a bit meant he was performing and a hackamore meant he was working. He ponied babies and yearlings, chased cows, bushwhacked across the desert, and did all kinds of things. He also carried me to a top ten placing in the nation at year's end. The consistent message always was, "Give the right response and you won't be bugged by bit or hackamore."

Bo is bred to work cattle. None of my six horses are good dressage prospects. They could certainly learn all the maneuvers but would never be competitive no matter how well they performed.

You could ask your horse to run as if both his life and yours depended on it, but try as he might, you probably couldn't win the Kentucky Derby. Even if Bo gave his utmost to the most skilled dressage trainer (which counts me out) he would not do well at any but the very beginning levels of dressage. Bo is athletically built for comfort and power with more muscle mass and less extension than called for in competitive dressage horses.

I pitched my goal of pursuing classical dressage out the window. There's no way I am going to tell Bo that the last seven years was a lie. Maintaining my relationship with Bo is more important than any rule of competition or lesson plan. I'm looking forward to more coaching - but the goal is no longer dressage. My goal is to build an even stronger relationship with Bo by making both of us more ABLE.

I have to remind myself that Bo never spent one month in a training program. Only one of our horses had the experience of being in progressive work five days a week for months and years on end. Asti was in my training barn for three years back when I was still fairly sound. Bo is willing, confident, and obedient – but he is not highly trained. How could he be? No one rides him except me and I wasn't in any shape to teach him. That joy IS our journey together.

If you find yourself getting too heavy on the reins or too aggressive with your spurs, stop to reassess your goal. Sometimes you need to change the objective of your riding session, change your training method or simply slow things down a whole bunch and take smaller steps. CHT places relationship above every other goal.

Perspective

The view from the top of a horse is not the same as the view from the ground. A frequent and common mistake is reaching conclusions without understanding the perspective or viewpoint that established the facts.

There is a lot of disagreement about Christian doctrine and a lot of disagreement among experts in the world of horses. How do you decide who is right and who is wrong? First you need to understand where they're coming from; their perspective.

- Which is right, a western headstall with a snaffle bit and rope reins or a full dressage bridle?

- Which is right, a cowboy hat or a helmet?

- Which is right, chaps or breeches?

- Which is right, western spurs with a three inch shank and bumpy rowels or simple English spurs with short curved shanks?

- Which is the right way to wear an English spur, curved up or curved down?

I've actually held up these objects and asked audiences this series of questions. The answers change as the audience changes. Does that really mean that what is right and what is wrong changes with the folks? Certainly not.

The point that matters in Christian Horse Training is that every question deals with a horse; the body, spirit, and soul of an equine as God made it. The trappings don't matter. A similar truth applies to the questions of Christian doctrine; every question or issue deals with a human and the One who created him or her. The trappings don't matter.

God establishes what is right and what is wrong. I doubt He has given the slightest notice to bridles, spurs, or equestrian wear. What is acceptable and what is not depends on the particular horse or the rules of some competition. Unfortunately, many people think that questions of tack, hoof care, attire, or training are "salvation" issues in the religion of Equus. The gauge of what is right and wrong with your horse is the condition of the relationship you share.

Promises Kept

"Some people don't understand the promises they're making when they make them," I said. "Right, of course.

But you keep the promise anyway. That's what love is. Love is keeping the promise anyway." - John Green

What do you call someone who tells you a lie? You call him a liar. What do you call someone who makes a promise but fails to keep it? You call him a liar.

It is quite astounding how many people testify to faith in known liars. The excuses range from "She may have lied to you, but she wouldn't lie to me!" to "She may have lied about this but that doesn't mean she would lie about anything really important!"

Liars are manipulators. They lie to sway, to convince, to persuade, to evade, or to prepare an ambush. Satan is the father of lies. God is truth. There is no middle ground.

There is a lie in every broken promise. Worthy leaders do not intentionally lie. Ever. No exceptions. Promises are not made unless there is overwhelming confidence that they can be kept.

Compartmentalization doesn't work

Trying to keep part of your life separate from any other part never works out well. The way you care for your horses testifies to the state of your relationship with God. Your behavior in church should be familiar to all who know you outside of the congregation. The horse you have at home is the same horse you haul to a show or ride on the trail.

There is nothing you can keep from God and any hole you leave in your horse's training will come back to bite you at

the worst possible moment. Horses are very willing
creatures, but what a horse is willing to do for you in the
safety of familiar surroundings has a lot to do with the
security of those surroundings. Take a horse away from
home and it will either place its trust in you or assume the
responsibility to watch out and react to danger in spite of
you.

Horses transformed by relationship do not discriminate
between home and not home. As long as the object of its
faith is present fear is not necessary. What could possibly
frighten you if God stands at your side?

> *"The Lord is my light and my salvation;*
> *Whom shall I fear?*
> *The Lord is the strength of my life;*
> *Of whom shall I be afraid?" – Psalm 27*

Have you ever wondered why God brings the same
problem back to you again and again? God will never force
open a door you shut to the Spirit, but He will faithfully
open another. Facing the same challenge over and over may
indicate that you have sealed some door against the power
of the Holy Spirit that prevents Him from dealing with
what is hidden.

If your horse keeps coming up with some resistance you
thought you had erased, it means the underlying problem is
still present. Peel away the layers one by one by asking the
question as each new layer is exposed; *Is the horse unable
or unwilling to do as I ask*?

Your commitment and ability to lead will eventually free

your horse from its hidden fears just as the Holy Spirit will for you.

Rationalization

The difference between transformative relationship and those that fall short is focus and commitment. Whenever one's concentration centers on "I, me, mine" relationship suffers, whether with God, horses, or one another.

Horses are the perfect partners for people pursuing the height of what is possible in relationship because they don't lie to themselves or each other. The problem most people have is that they don't always know when they're lying to themselves. The primary work of psychologists is helping patients recognize the truth about themselves.

Oswald Chambers sums up the nature of how a shift in focus and the practice of rationalization (making excuses) happens even among more mature Christians. Chambers calls it *spiritual leakage*. When faced with a result that falls short of expectation and weariness or commitment begins to wear thin some may say,

"I have been stretching myself a bit too much, standing on tiptoe and trying to look like God instead of being an ordinary humble person."

or

"Well, after all, was I not a bit too pretentious? Was I not taking a stand a bit too high? Well, I suppose I was expecting too much."

There is a huge difference between pursuing righteousness and believing that you can do what God can do. Dumbing down what you think are overly high standards is a form of pride, and completely different from the humility of total reliance on God. The former is the rejection of God's authority to set standards as well as judge whether they have been met. It sets the wisdom of the world over relationship with God. The latter, humility borne of faith and submission to Jesus Christ, brings with it peace, assurance, and security. God establishes both the rules and the grading scale. *"Be still and know that I AM God."* - Psalm 46:10

The same temptation may also come when you think you're stuck with your horse, when results fall short of expectation, or you become weary and your commitment begins to wear thin.

The first conversation you have to have with yourself is to honestly understand what you were trying to accomplish. Is your goal one of *doing* or *being*? Are you frustrated that you're not mastering specific training goals or failing to establish a meaningful relationship with your horse?

"Well, maybe I've been aiming at too high a goal. I'm not a professional trainer. Maybe I'm trying to be something I'm not."

"My horse doesn't have a reining pedigree. Maybe I've been expecting too much, trying to put a good handle on him. Maybe he is really just a pasture horse."

Are you more concerned with being a trainer or a worthy master? Is the problem one of ability or willingness? Yours or the horse's?

Help your horse become more able or motivate him to become more willing. Is it time to adjust your training or relationship program or move on to another horse? There is no ceiling on what is possible in relationship with a horse as long as you are both fully committed.

Correction

"Correction is not for the detection of faults, but in order to make perfect." – Oswald Chambers

There is a big difference between properly applied correction and a crutch. Building confidence in a horse or human depends on how well the principles and application of correction are understood and applied. Whether human, equine, or canine – the practice of employing frequent and unceasing correction to maintain proper direction, focus, or balance will eventually cease to be a tool for 'making perfect' and devolve into a crutch of dependency.

Constant supervision may be appropriate to introduce new concepts, to teach, or to communicate precision. What is important to note is how the process of learning deliberately and predictably moves from the macro to the micro. Early lessons teach broad concepts. Over time and practice lessons gear toward refinement and self-correction.

Whether a child learning to write the alphabet, a middle-schooler learning to play the slide trombone, or a horse learning to carry a rider forward in a straight line, lessons graduate from the simple and singular to those more conceptual and integrated.

Transformative relationship is just that. You don't bounce from your old man to your new based upon the circumstances of the moment. With the possible exception of multiple personality disorders there are no separations within a person. The person you are at home is the same person you are in public. The face you present to your spouse is the same you wear to church on Sunday. Your behavior may appear different but you are the same. The fact that your behavior is inconsistent is evidence that you need to spend a little more time with your Master.

Horses often act differently at home from how they do at a show. Even at home a horse may behave one way in the indoor arena and quite differently in the big pasture or riding through the woods. Does that mean the horse has multiple personality disorder? No.

What it means is the horse is more confident in some places or situations than in others. That tells you that its confidence in the leader is not as great as it might be – faith and relationship is not as powerful as circumstances. There is work to be done, but not to change the horse – but rather to strengthen leadership by working on maintaining a correct focus even when the horse is tempted to distraction.

CONSISTENCY AND COMMITMENT

Any discussion of leadership characteristics must include the essentials of consistency and commitment. Some folks say the Bible is inconsistent. Jesus tells the eleven in Mark 16:15 to go out and *preach the gospel to all the world.* Yet in Matthew 7:6 Jesus tells us not *to cast holy pearls before swine.*

Here's one that might raise some eyebrows:

> *"Do not answer a fool according to his folly,*
> *Lest you also be like him." – Proverbs 26:4*

followed by,

> *"Answer a fool according to his folly,*
> *Lest he be wise in his own eyes." – Proverbs 26:5*

On the surface these verses appear to clearly contradict one another. I assure you they do not.

Learning the subtleties involved in moving your horse's body by changing the way you use your own frustrates many novice riders. What do you think about these statements?

To turn your horse left use your right leg.

To turn your horse left use your left leg.

Are they contradictory? Confusing to many, certainly, but they are neither inconsistent nor do they contradict one another.

Whether you use your right leg, left leg, or both legs depends entirely on the position of your horse's body when you decide you wish to turn left. There is no single correct cue to get a horse to turn. Some horses turn left from a direct left rein while others turn left when an indirect rein touches the right side of the neck.

One answers a fool to the extent that it is profitable to him and brings glory to God. In some cases the folly of the fool indicates he is unable or unwilling to listen to reason so no answer should be given. On other occasions the folly of the fool suggests he may be open to wisdom and then it is best to correct his error with truth.

When eyes are open and ears unstopped preach the gospel. When eyes are closed and ears refuse to hear, resist the urge to cast holy pearls before swine. Discernment is required when dealing with fools and training horses.

There are no contradictions in the Bible. Any failure to understand how two verses or concepts connect is not in God's Word but your understanding. Faith in the inerrancy of God calms any doubt, and you may rest assured that when God wants you to understand He will provide wisdom and discernment. He makes you able.

Horses with great faith in their masters may register curiously different messages from you but, like New

Creations in Christ, they put aside any concern because they believe that if it becomes necessary for them to know, the master will provide understanding. The ability to provide consistent messages is learned from experience, trial and error, and depends on your level of commitment to being a worthy leader.

The further along you journey in relationship with Christ the more consistent you will become in relationship with your horse. The application section of this book will help you become more consistent and precise in the way you communicate with your horse – or anyone else.

Aqql or Apple?

Setting performance standards requires precision and consistency.

Before little kids learn to read they have to know what letters are. In order to write children have to learn how to form letters by copying lines on a piece of paper with a big fat pencil until they can consistently reproduce the lines correctly and recognize which letter is which. Afterwards the children learn how letters combine to form words.

That system of learning is the same trainers use with horses and the Holy Spirit uses with us. Everyone starts at the beginning with the basics. The earliest lessons have to do with showing up, learning to focus and remain attentive in class, and then offering obedience to perform the tasks of each lesson.

In early stages of learning to read and write simply reciting the alphabet is a great success. Once mastered verbally another huge accomplishment is writing all twenty-six letters. More advanced students learn to combine individual letters into words and associate written words with a person, place, thing, or concept.

Mom and Dad are rightly thrilled when little Susie and Ralphie first learn to sing the ABC song. Susie and Ralphie earn more praise and shiny gold stars when they learn to write the letters correctly. Then the day comes when Susie and Ralphie write the word that describes that shiny red fruit – aqql.

Okay, we all know that aqql isn't quite correct and the word should be apple. But as a first attempt this is pretty good. The crayon picture of an apple underscored with the letters "aqql" is proudly displayed on the door of the refrigerator and the house hums with delight.

Consistent Standards

A few months later Susie and Ralphie have learned that "aqql" isn't correct and that the juicy red fruit is an "apple." A new picture goes up on the refrigerator and all is right with the world.

Would you think it strange if Susie and Ralphie correctly spelled out the word apple 30 times and then reverted back to "aqql"? Should Mom and Dad be concerned or gloss over the spelling shorthand because Susie and Ralphie already got it right 30 times? Why get excited about the thirty-first?

Most parents would go right back to the spelling drills. If Susie and Ralphie know the difference between aqql and apple and still spell the word incorrectly then they don't consider proper spelling very important. If Susie and Ralphie don't realize they got it wrong then they need more help to master the lesson. Once a standard is set – in this instance the correct spelling of apple – is there any circumstance that makes it acceptable for the kids to spell it wrong? Why would established standards be ignored?

Horse trainers ignore standards all the time. I do it myself. Christians ignore standards all the time. I do it myself. Why do we let ourselves get away with it? Is it because we don't recognize what we're doing or because we don't care enough about that particular standard to be faithful? Are we unable or unwilling to behave correctly?

The main reason standards fail is lack of commitment. It takes practice and repetition to achieve and maintain excellence. You must care enough to do the work. There's a big difference between getting your horse to do a left lead and teaching your horse to consistently execute a correct left lead departure softly and quietly.

Too many of us get our horses to pick up a left lead a few times and think we're done. Does your horse really know his leads? Well, it depends on how you define leads. If the only criterion applied regards footfall then it's not too difficult. But if *knowing leads* involves proper body position from muzzle to hocks, soft obedience to all aids, ridability of speed and direction, and establishing a firm foundation for higher order maneuvers - no horse can master the left lead in a week. Or a month.

Teaching a lead begins the same way Susie and Ralphie

learned to spell apple. First they learned the letters, then words, then connected a word to an object. Once the children learned that the juicy red fruit meant *apple* nothing less should ever be accepted again. That is the end of aqql. No more.

First your horse has to learn to carry a rider at the lope (canter) with enough balance and confidence to do so safely. Next the horse needs to learn a cue that means move into a lope. Most horses trot into a canter in the early stages of their education. Once the horse understands what you want he must be both able and willing to reliably offer the proper response.

Once your horse consistently picks up a lope when you ask he must learn that his left lead is different from his right lead. Some horses figure it out quickly while others must first learn a far higher degree of specific body part control before they can understand the difference.

Every time you raise the bar the standard changes permanently. Allowing your horse to trot into a lope after you taught him not to accepts *aqql*. Why? Is the standard *aqql* or *apple*?

"Oh, he knows the difference. It doesn't matter if he did it wrong this time. After all, we're not working on leads today."

So, as long as the quiz isn't a spelling test then it's okay for Ralphie to spell apple *aqql*? Of course not. Why then do we permit our horses to make a mistake without being corrected? Only one of two reasons, we are either unable to make the correction or unwilling to do so. Since we taught the horse how to do it properly to begin with the problem isn't one of ability. It must be a lack of commitment. If getting the proper lead when cued correctly isn't important enough to fix, you just lowered the standard. If the rider doesn't care about proper leads, why should the horse?

Susie and Ralphie thought spelling apple correctly was important until they did it wrong a few times without consequence. Unfortunately, when you get your horse to the lesson or show and he messes up you may correct him far more harshly because "he knows how to do it" and you assume he is purposefully choosing not to obey. Horses are punished for rider error thousands of times every day. Are you guilty?

Many horse owners call their horses in from the pasture, throw on a saddle and bridle they happen to own, and pop off down the lane. If a physical, behavioral, or riding problem crops up the owners are motivated to seek additional knowledge.

Horse folks learn about hoof care, saddle fitting, the proper selection of bits, and how to properly feed and manage horses because they have a passion or because they experience a problem. Once a horse recovers from lameness due to bad shoeing, back pain caused by poor saddle fit, or colic from a poor diet, the owner knows far more than she used to.

Is it acceptable to go back to bad hoof care, the saddle that caused the injury, and cheap nasty feed that caused colic? Certainly not. The standards of care have changed because there is a new level of understanding and accountability.

When I was about eight years old I gleefully rode a pony at a fast clip down the drive beside a southern Minnesota soybean field. I don't remember what I did, but my uncle stopped me short and curtly told me to either get off the pony or ride her correctly. I learned to groom, saddle, harness, ride, and drive well enough to satisfy my uncle. I adored him for that!

I am accountable to a far higher standard of care when I saddle my horses today than when I saddled my first pony more than a half century ago. Thankfully my uncle didn't let me do anything that harmed the ponies.

As you progress further along in your journey with Christ – and with your horse – standards will change. And once set, standards must be maintained.

Should we hold everyone to the same standard of horsemanship? No. The journey of joy is progressive. We discover more about how to care for and teach our horses as we expand our understanding of what may be possible in relationship with our horses.

Once you know how to spell apple correctly the standard must be enforced. No one ever achieved excellence with horses without failing a horse somewhere along the way. None of us will make it to heaven without failing someone we love – including our Savior – many times. All error is not sin and some sins are only recognized in the rear view mirror. If we knew at the time that the bit hurt our horse we wouldn't have used it. If we knew that an old behavior violated a commandment from God we would not have done what we did.

What counts against us in our most precious relationships are the things we didn't do that we knew we should and the things we did do that we knew we shouldn't. Faith is built on standards, trust, consistency, and commitment. Fail in any of them and fear wiggles into the opening.

Whatever skill you teach your horse you are obligated to maintain unless you intend to forever excuse the horse from performing it correctly in the future. Whatever the Holy Spirit convicts you of becomes a new standard by which you will be judged. *Not only do you know that it is sin but you know that He knows that you know that He knows.*

Commitment

The Ten Commandments have not softened with time. For the worldly the definition of 'commitment' is far more elastic than it used to be, but not for those who pursue transformative relationship with Christ or a horse.

Are you committed?

- "Yes, unless a deal breaker pops up."
- "Yes, as long as…"
- "Yes, if…"
- *"Yes -- no matter what."*

Only the final answer is worthy of a New Creation in Christ. It isn't possible to gauge the level of someone else's commitment until the fruit is seen and evaluated. Sometimes it isn't possible to know exactly what our own level of commitment is until an obstacle, problem, or crisis appears and is overcome.

"*No matter what*" means exactly that. No deal breakers and no excuses. Promising to love until death you do part is unconditional. There is no second option.

The mere presence of an observable sin neither proves nor disproves whether one has a true and abiding love for Jesus Christ. The mere presence of an observable error in how a horse owner manages or rides her horse neither proves nor disproves whether she seeks transformative relationship with her horse or not.

Knowing something is a sin and understanding that what you're doing is a sin is not always the same thing. Most of us agree that animal abuse is a sin. I am absolutely confident that God has a special line of judgment for all who abuse animals or children. It is not a line you want to find yourself in.

There are hundreds of wonderful horse trainers who abused a horse early in their career. But they didn't know it was abuse at the time. Would I do a few things differently? Absolutely.

Making a commitment to Christ, to a spouse, to children, or to a horse means that you will do everything in your power to make the right promises and keep them. Continuing to learn more about worthy leadership reveals the error of past ways. The more time you spend in God's Word under the instruction of the Holy Spirit the more you recognize past mistakes.

Christian Horse Training is a commitment without reserve in the same way. New Creations are all in. Anything withheld from Christ gives fear an opportunity. There are no part-timers or temporary workers in the family of God. Christian horse trainers pursue right relationship with complete commitment 100% of the time – without exception. Does that mean our execution will be flawless? No. But our commitment is unwavering.

Part-time leaders are fakes. Their promises may or may not be lies. Horses are smart enough to tell the difference and you can't fool God (Galatians 6:7). True commitments cannot be broken without destruction. Not only is the one who broke it guilty and the bonds of relationship severed, but the spirits of others involved will be corrupted, crushed, or broken.

Teach a child that his father lies and the child is changed forever. Teach a horse that the faith he has in his owner is a lie and it becomes difficult to pull faith from the ashes or accept worthy leadership from a new master. Teach a Christian that God's Word is inconsistent or situational and faith that saves disappears.

Jesus never fails and God's Word is always true. The important point is that the legacy of broken commitments extend far beyond the day or circumstance.

People truly committed to God, horses, or others are willing to change themselves in order to change the quality of relationship. Can you imagine any change greater than God becoming a human baby?

Sometimes folks come over to ride with me because they ran out of ideas trying to fix a problem with their horse. Seldom is the problem what they thought it was. The culprit is usually poor leadership with inconsistent and contradictory lessons. Horses that don't have a solid foundation built upon predictable, purposeful and positive outcomes respond with anxiety, aggression, or simply quit trying at all.

After an hour of easy work doing basic exercises riders often begin to see changes in their horse; the horse becomes soft, obedient, relaxed, and focused. Through a series of simple progressive steps a glimmer of hope and trust starts to glow in renewed relationship between horse and rider.

This is the place where the truth of commitment is revealed. The rider is getting the result she wanted and the horse is grateful and content. Most troubles are solved by slowly and methodically rebuilding the crumbled foundation of relationship until it is strong enough to build on once again.

When a rider is totally committed to transformative relationship, he or she is happy to continue working at the speed and level the horse requires to overcome past issues and gain renewed faith. The journey itself must be the gift the rider seeks, not competing at a barrel race or horse show next weekend. Enough must be enough.

Some riders will do whatever it takes to transform a stiff, wary, and unbalanced horse into one that is confident, capable, responsive, and reliable -- even if it means foregoing events and more exciting things than basic lessons and practice, practice, practice. Every great artist, athlete, and musician had to give up other interests and pursuits in order to practice, practice, practice. The basic question is one of simple commitment: What is most important to you?

If relationship with your horse isn't the most important reason you have a horse, that's perfectly acceptable. But you must still be a good steward and you must not lie to your horse by promising something you have no intention of giving. God does not look favorably on neglect, abuse, or lying.

I am always saddened when a rider gets the result she (or he) wants from a horse who forgives again and again, yet decides to go back to her (his) same old habits. The commitment simply isn't sufficient and maybe "aqql" is okay after all. That's not a problem if the rider is honest and does not promise her horse deeper relationship.

Commitment isn't just a major element of transformative relationship – it is the engine that drives everything else. Power, skills, ability, and accomplishment are of little use to a scared kid or insecure horse. I don't believe it's possible to correctly divide a horse's *can't* from its *won't* unless you know and care for the horse on a personal basis. Horses are dominated, coerced, punished, and abused because a trainer or owner thinks they are being stubborn, stupid, or hateful when the truth is the horses are simply unable to do as asked.

Commitment to another requires some amount of self denial. Lots of folks are willing to read books, watch

DVDs, attend clinics, and take a few lessons about proper horse training. They dabble and splash around the edges of the pond of transformative relationship but refuse to go all in. They'll risk getting a toe or foot wet, but they are unwilling to dive into the center.

New Creations in Christ make a complete commitment. They are changed. It isn't possible to put on and take off the mantle of Spirit like a wet saddle blanket. "Now I'm available; now I'm not." Commitment to Christ and to CHT is a decision to walk a different path than you did before. There is no option to reverse course or detour when something tempting comes along.

Distractions

Success is the product of a foundation built of habits that promote and predict actions that lead to success. Distractions divert your focus from what you intended to concentrate on to something that you did not intend to think about or do. Distractions seldom register to your conscious mind until the deed is done and you realize you're not where you intended to be.

> *"The unmarried woman cares about the things of the Lord, that she may be holy both in body and in spirit. But she who is married cares about the things of the world—how she may please her husband. And this I say for your own profit, not that I may put a leash on you, but for what is proper, and that you may serve the Lord without distraction." – 1 Corinthians 7:34-35*

The observation Paul shares speaks to unity of purpose, focus, goal, and pursuit. It is only possible to have one main goal. If you think about the concept of goal as an actual destination you cannot have two. You will arrive at one and fail to reach the other or you will make it to neither because you are unable to make decisions that bring you closer to either goal.

Recently I presented a program on being equally yoked to an equine-based ministry for women. One of the exercises involved two ladies, one on either end of an eight-foot pole with a light harrow attached by a ring sliding along the center of the pole. As expected, the team pulled in unison to get their load through a small obstacle course. Before they set off I had given each lady a note with directions to the finish line.

Hearts Desire Ministry. Photo – Shirley Cook

Everything went along smoothly with a few adjustments to balance the load as turns were executed. Then the team hit a wall. One lady pulled to the south while the other pulled to the north. The team members were not allowed to speak with each other and they exchanged looks of surprise, annoyance, and then amusement.

What happened next will not predictably happen in all instances. Rather than give up on crossing the finish line both ladies pulled and gestured with elbows and chins to see if the other could be influenced to follow her lead. Neither one gave in. The team separated and the stronger lady pulled the load to her finish line while the other lady made it to her finish line in one piece but without the harrow.

By this time it was apparent to everyone that each lady was given directions to a different finish line. Goals cannot be achieved if they require you to be in two places at the same time or to pursue two equal but incompatible goals.

LEADERSHIP FAILURE

When a Christian faces some dilemma about what to do or not to do there is usually an emotional element. The normal state of contentment, peace, and deep faith is disrupted by anxiety, anger, or aggression. Either the battle is about understanding the choice itself or a conscious (or unconscious) desire to rationalize making the wrong choice without feeling guilty.

- Is it wrong to spend the family's vacation fund on a new car?

- Should we have a child before we graduate from college?

- Is it okay to let my teenagers play violent video games?

- My wife wants me to stop drinking beer, but I only have a few on Saturday. Should I quit?

- My son is coming for a visit next month and wants to bring his girlfriend. Should we let them sleep together in our home?

- My health isn't what it used to be because I just don't like to exercise and who cares if I'm a little heavy?

- The Lord expects me to spend time alone with Him every morning. I stayed up really late last night watching a movie. Surely it's okay to miss this morning because I'm just so tired.

- One of my friends is going fishing Sunday morning. I said I would cover for the Sunday school teacher. Why shouldn't someone else cover for me so I can spend time with my friend? After all, I'm not the real teacher anyway.

Anyone who's participated in these very normal internal debates recognizes the feelings of guilt, disquiet, and resentment that come along for the ride. Choosing to obey is a bumpier road than reflexive obedience because you recognize that the actual choice is between doing as Jesus asks and telling your Savior, "No."

Your spirit lets you know the instant you get out into the weeds of debate about what you should or shouldn't do. The burden gets heavier and the yoke becomes a drag on your back. Make the wrong decision and you can go fishing, drink another beer on Saturday, have a baby you can't support and have it *your way*. But the road will not be smooth and the peace that passeth understanding will recede into memory.

Once you obey however, the reward is immediate! Your spirit lifts, your peace returns, and the beauty of relationship with Christ returns to bless all you see and do. God will not make you do the right thing. Eventually you cease trying to indulge yourself because there is nothing better than walking peaceably with your God. Everything else pales in comparison. [Micah 6:8]

Automatic (reflexive) obedience is an easy burden and a very light yoke because you don't even know you're carrying it.

CHT seeks the gift of obedience from the horse. Making a horse do what you want may satisfy for a moment, but the only foundation laid is rough and ugly. CHT does not threaten dominance; it promises a light yoke and easy burden. In return the horse receives peace, security, affection, affiliation, and becomes more than a horse through right relationship with a committed, worthy master.

Horses also learn to obey reflexively by experience and blossoming relationship. They don't have to consciously consider whether or not to say "Yes" to your request or cue. They do so automatically without any real thought. In the dance of transformative relationship the leader leads and the horse follows seamlessly, without making conscious decisions. They just go with the spiritual and physical flow.

- Do you have to catch your horse or does he come up to greet you?

- Does your horse respect your personal space?

- Do you have to drag your horse around with the lead rope or is it more of a decoration and emergency brake?

- Is your horse patient when groomed and saddled?

- Does your horse wait for you or walk all over you?

- Does your horse tell you what it will and will not do?

- When you're riding your horse does it pay more attention to grass, other horses, or some cow a quarter-mile away than to you?

- Is your horse spooky, pushy, or numb?

- Does your horse respond to cues you aren't even aware you gave?

- Can you ride your horse without a bridle and bit?

- Are you afraid of your horse? Is he afraid of you?

If your horse gets angry, aggressive, or anxious there is a problem that requires you to step up. If you get angry, aggressive, or anxious working with your horse you have a problem that requires you to step up.

Horses committed to relationship build a habit of obedience. You ask, they respond. Like people, whenever a horse has to make a decision about whether or not to do as asked there often is some degree of emotional upset. You provide food, water, shelter, love, companionship, security, and serve as the herd leader every horse seeks from birth.

Decisions about **what** to do are issues of communication or ability; a decision about **whether or not** to obey is the difference between willingness and rejection. Horses that reject their herd leader put themselves in jeopardy. Their peace is broken and fear creeps in.

It is possible to ride a horse without saddle or bridle. It is possible for a rider to simply think, *Trot out to the tree* and the horse trots out to the tree. The rider never had to give a conscious cue and the horse never had to consider whether or not to obey. The master thought and the pair moved in response. It's not only possible, but it happens – I've done it myself. I expect many of you who read this have as well. Because we have tasted what is possible we continue to pursue more. The journey continues.

Reflexive obedience grows until horse and rider work together without really knowing where one stops and the other begins. Reflexive obedience in Christians begins at the moment of rebirth. The gift of such obedience blesses you because the depth of love and relationship with Jesus Christ grows. As a New Creation in Christ there really is a place of connection within you where it is impossible to know where you stop and the Holy Spirit begins.

It is a miracle of mercy and grace.

Leadership Failure and Accountability

There is no better mirror by which you may evaluate the state of your relationship with God than the present state of relationship you have with your horse. If your horse is obstinate there's a good chance you're obstinate before

God. If your horse is stiff-necked and stubborn, you may also have a stiff neck unwilling to bend before God's authority. If your horse is easily distracted it's possible you may also be easily distracted. If your horse is steadfast and reliable you may be equally steadfast and reliable.

Would you agree that any complexity or difficulty any person experiences in relationship with God is his or her fault? If not, then you must believe God is at fault and the person is just an innocent victim.

Would you agree that any complexity or difficulty a human experiences in relationship with horses is the fault of the person? If not, then you believe the horse is at fault and the person is just an innocent victim.

Leadership Failure

In the simplest sense failure is always the fault of humans; never God and never the horse. However, common sense tells you that not all situations are so simple. Other people often contribute to the equation and mess up what could and should have been wonderful relationship between a horse and human. Your horse may have some serious problems and habits that you did not cause. But they started somewhere and are most likely the fault of a previous person in the horse's life.

Unless you claimed a horse at the moment of birth or personally brought it in from the wild, there is a high probability that the horse already has experienced "human." Such contact may have been positive and serves as a firm foundation for the relationship you hope to enjoy with it. In too many cases, however, the horse that's out grazing in your pasture may have already learned not to trust humans - even to fight or run away.

The relationship you have with Jesus Christ may be influenced by what others have said and done or by what other people have NOT said and done. People in positions of authority sometimes provide wonderful support and insight into God's Word and the pursuit of relationship with Him. It is also commonplace for authority figures to preach what is not true, causing others to mistrust the Bible itself or convict God's character based on human wisdom.

"Therefore let us not judge one another anymore, but rather resolve this, not to put a stumbling block or a cause to fall in our brother's way." – Romans 14:13

Most Christians have met someone who said they soured on church and Christianity because of the "hypocritical" behavior of self-professed believers or other seemingly harsh or hateful messages. Humans, like horses, learn not to trust God because of what others say or do – they may even fight or run away.

The road you walk with Christ probably includes a few potholes and burned bridges. God didn't put them there; all roadwork that destroys is the work of man. When God burns a bridge it's because it was a temptation to lead you away from Him.

Any problem you have with God is your problem. Forget the past because it is past. Move forward. You can't train a horse without forward movement and you can't improve your walk with the Lord unless you are willing to move onward, not backward.

Signs of Leadership Failure

The signs of leadership failure are usually visible and observable. Negative emotions can be a symptom of leadership failure or a failure of followership; an unwillingness to be led. Whether the relationship in question is between two humans or a human and horse, there are three basic signs of leadership failure:

1. Anger
2. Anxiety
3. Aggression

The product of transformative relationship - the visible result of proper focus and obedience - is peace. New Creations in Christ understand this "peace that passes all understanding" (Philippians 4:7). Christians secure in Christ are not undone by the trials and hardships of living in the world. They are aware but undaunted. Likewise, horses secure in relationship with a worthy leader/master recognize noisy, flappy, difficult challenges, but they do not run.

In both instances, with Christians and secure horses, the natural horrors of life become either annoyances or opportunities. Annoyances are tolerated until the dust of the moment can be brushed off the feet and you move one (Matthew 10:14). Puzzles, predicaments, and true obstacles present the opportunity to overcome, to grow, to testify, to learn, and to test one's faith. Faith is strengthened each time God brings us through in victory.

"We trust not because "a God" exists, but because this God exists." – CS Lewis

When tested, faith grows. The evidence of faith is peace, contentment, serenity, and hope. Anger, anxiety, and aggression are caused by the same emotion – fear.

It's easy to make the connection between anxiety and fear. The words themselves can be used as synonyms for each other. Unresolved anger is like a pressure cooker. Without a way to cool the steam it will blow into aggression.

The wrath of God is expressed as anger many times in the Bible. Righteous anger is a response to the disrespectful, senseless, or hurtful act of another. Anger is also a defense mechanism used by foolish or manipulative people. The most common emotional reactions to injustice are anger and sorrow. Anxiety is just another word for fear.

Most of you probably have plenty of experience with anger and fear. Recognizing and managing aggression in a positive way can be a bit trickier.

Aggression – Pushiness or War

Aggressive behavior in horses sometimes manifests as pushiness; a lack of respect that invades your personal space or recognizes your cue but purposefully ignores it. At other times aggression is demonstrated by a horse that insists on not only having a vote, but veto power as well.

The worst kind of aggressive behavior is physical, where a horse actually threatens you with its head, teeth, feet, or body slam. If mildly aggressive behaviors are not properly resolved they often escalate over time. Actions some horse owners think are signs of confidence and boldness in their horse may really be aggressive in nature.

Many people have trouble figuring out the difference between assertiveness and aggression in other humans. Sometimes we have the same problem trying to nail down the truth about our own motives or actions. How would you answer these questions?

- Is using a loud tone of voice aggressive or assertive?

- Is pointing a finger at someone aggressive or assertive?

- Is banging your fist on a table aggressive or assertive?

- Is standing really close to someone else aggressive or assertive?

- Is looking directly into someone's eyes aggressive or assertive?

- Is touching someone's arm aggressive or assertive?

- Is walking away during a disagreement aggressive or assertive?

- Is drawing a "line in the sand" aggressive or assertive?

- Is an ultimatum aggressive or assertive?

There isn't a correct universal answer to any of these questions. The answer for each one is, "It depends."

The difference between Assertive and Aggressive

Are horses that buck, rear, and kick behaving badly? All horses run, buck, and kick. The only way to determine if running, bucking, or kicking is appropriate or not is putting the behavior in context.

The important question is "Why?" What caused the horse to respond in such a physical way? Is it just expressing himself or reacting to something another horse or a person did?

Unless you know why the horse bucked, reared or kicked it's difficult to respond correctly. Horses rear, buck, and kick when they play. Horses rear, buck and kick when they are attacked. Horses rear, buck, and kick when they're trained to. Horses also rear, buck, and kick when they are being forced to move and don't recognize any other option.

Characteristics of Aggressive Behavior

- Aggression is reactive.

- Aggression is evidence of weakness.

- Aggression is a sign of imbalance.

- Aggression is destructive (intentionally or not).

- Aggression has an emotional basis (unless it is drug induced).

Characteristics of Assertive Behavior

- Assertive behavior is responsive.

- Assertive behavior is evidence of strength.

- Assertive behavior is balanced and proportional.

- Assertive behavior is constructive.

- Assertive behavior is considered and measured.

As master, trainer, or leader it is your responsibility to know what caused your horse to act out. Unless a horse is good-naturedly playing with other horses or is trick-trained you must respond to kicking, rearing, or bucking swiftly, proportionately, unemotionally, and constructively.

You are responsible for the state of relationship you enjoy with your horse and with God. Not only are you accountable for your horse's behavior but you are accountable for how you respond to it. Do you tend to be assertive or aggressive?

Raising your voice to a horse is seldom appropriate unless you are giving a short staccato message like "Quit!" because you're thirty feet down the breezeway. When would you consider it appropriate for someone to yell at you? The only example that occurs to me would be some short staccato words of warning – "Look out!" or "Loose horse!"

Examine the characteristics of both aggressive and assertive behavior. They are active responses or reactions. The other option is passive response which is inactive. When training horses and building foundations of relationship you will generally choose to use either a passive or assertive response. Aggression is a display of negative emotions. There is no place for negative emotions in relationship with a horse, or with anyone else for that matter.

Jesus was despised, denied, rejected, and crucified. Jesus wept, He cleared the temple, and He lived for three years with men who didn't understand Him. The example our Lord gives us is the perfect balance of authority and humility.

> *"[Jesus] had no need that anyone should testify*
> *of man, for He knew what was in man."– John 2:25*

Jesus knew the hearts and minds of all men. He responded accordingly. All who offer worthy leadership to a horse are expected to know about *what is in a horse*. No one will ever know all there is to know about horses because the learning process never stops unless you decide to quit.

You need to learn how to read and predict a horse's reaction to what you do. You have to know why you do what you do. If you're about to put pressure on a horse's hip, why? If you're going to pick up the left snaffle rein and apply pressure, why?

All we do is in the sight of God. When we are alone in His presence we are accountable. When we interact with other people we are accountable. When we accept some blessing of the world God created we are accountable, and for anything we do with a child or animal we are even more accountable.

Is your horse's behavior aggressive or assertive? Is yours?

Aggression is a sign of leadership failure. If your horse reacts aggressively it is your fault. If you react aggressively to your horse it is your fault. In that case the failure is in both your leadership and your own followership to your Master and Lord.

Aggression is a sign of weakness. Your horse should grow stronger and bolder through right relationship with you. Your own increasing strength is the product of being the child of a holy, omnipotent God.

Aggression is a sign of imbalance. Faith cannot co-exist with imbalance. Seek balance in your own life and extend the blessing to your horse as well. If you're overly emotional, out of balance, weak and indecisive, then you will be hard-pressed to keep the promises you make your horse.

"He has shown you, O man, what is good; And what does the LORD require of you but to do justly, to love mercy, and to walk humbly with your God?" – Micah 6:8

Hands of mercy may be assertive or passive, but grace is never aggressive. Just as darkness and light cannot co-exist it also impossible for mercy to be applied by a hand powered by weakness or negative emotion. Mercy may reveal an uncomfortable truth, habit, or behavior, but mercy and grace never destroy the foundations of right relationship.

Children learning to color must first master the motor skills and understanding that permits sufficient control of the crayon so the color remains on a page of paper without spreading to the floor, walls, or clothing. That first brilliant mastery of the crayon is rewarded and frequently given a place on the refrigerator gallery of honor. Remember *aqql*?

With practice and instruction children learn to concentrate; leaning to control the motion of their hands to keep the tip of the crayon within the outline of big shapes on the page. Simply staying on the page is no longer accepted as the definition of success. Correction is given when the color almost runs off the page, then progresses until the child learns how to keep the color inside the shape.

If a child's hand is always grabbed the instant the tip of the crayon strays from the shape to be colored, she will never learn to control the mark herself. The hand of the teacher changes from one offering constructive correction to one that functions as a crutch of limitation. Correction is the method used to communicate failure to achieve a goal, however small. The word *correction* has gotten a bad rap in recent decades because it draws attention to less than perfect performance.

Correction makes it possible for a child or horse to refine basic skills until muscle-memory, habit, and repetition yield excellent and consistent results. Correction is intended to make perfect, never to punish.

Let's discuss something more concrete than relationships to grasp the proper context of correction. Leave emotion aside and get technical. Let's talk about building the foundation of a building.

Generally you don't start laying a foundation without some vision of what the completed building or structure will be. Whether a retaining wall or cathedral, the beginning always dictates the outcome and vice versa. Unless you know what you're building you can't measure a proper foundation.

The analogy of building the foundation of a building and foundations of relationship parallel one another well, but we'll limit the extent of comparison to the matter at hand – correction.

Imagine that the ground has been excavated properly and is ready for the first course of brick. With a clean, level beginning the first course laid should be clean and level. Each brick rests on a firm foundation of earth, concrete, or stone.

Assuming the bricks are uniform and the mortar joints between each brick are the same width it is probable that the second course will be laid successfully. Bricks are methodically added by masons until the foundation begins to take shape.

As the foundation rises a problem appears. The top of the foundation is no longer level. The sides are not plumb. What should be done? A master mason is called in to diagnose the problem and recommend a solution.

After careful inspection the master mason points out where a small change caused by style differences between masons resulted in inconsistent mortar joints. What began as a small variance now manifested itself with a foundation unable to support the building. Should the error be corrected by taking the foundation back to the point where the problem started or should the builders simply design supports to keep it propped up?

Should the general contractor correct the problem or apply a crutch? A support will be unsightly and work until the weight of the building causes the weak foundation to fail. The building will collapse. Fixing the foundation will take longer and be costly, but the building will stand securely.

What can we learn from this example?

- Corrections are positive.

- Those who build foundations should be qualified.

- Deficiencies may be corrected or crutched.

- The integrity of a foundation determines ultimate success.

A small error or void in a foundation will always cause bigger troubles down the road. Either what was built will collapse or what is possible to build will be severely curtailed. This is true when building structures, training horses, or educating children. Leave a hole in a horse's basic training and it always comes back at the least opportune time.

> *"For whom the* LORD *loves He corrects, Just as a father the son in whom he delights." – Proverbs 3:12*

Correction is the gift of a worthy leader. Crutches are shortcuts that, in the end, cause what strength and potential that once existed to fail. Putting a brace on a leg eventually weakens the structures intended to support it. Like faith itself, muscles strengthen when tested or wither from disuse.

CHT BASIC COMMANDS

"For I also am a man under authority, having soldiers under me. And I say to this one, 'Go,' and he goes; and to another, 'Come,' and he comes; and to my servant, 'Do this,' and he does it." – Matthew 8:9

God wants the same three things from me that I want from my horses; to (1) Show up, (2) Focus, and (3) Offer obedience. The foundations of Christian Horse Training continue by comparing the basic commands Jesus gave to His disciples with the four basic commands we give to our horses:

- Come
- Follow
- Yield
- Go

Obedience is only possible if the opportunity exists to not obey. Jesus will never force you to do anything. To following His example properly means that we issue direction or make commands without force; at liberty, with a slack rope, or with hands that assist rather than accuse.

Come

> *"So He said, 'Come.' And when Peter had come down out of the boat, he walked on the water to go to Jesus."*
> *– Matthew 14:29*

"Come" may be used as either an invitation or a command. In either case it is only perfectly used with an open hand. "Come" is seldom associated with a yank or physical pull.

"Would you like to come?" is an invitation.

"Will you come?" is a question.

"Please come." Is a direct request.

"COME." is a command.

Come is a significant command. Obedience requires the horse to make a response of both body and will. "Come" never involves pulling. A horse cannot offer to "Come" if there is no choice other than compliance or being dragged forward.

Baber and Patrick

Follow

> *"My sheep hear My voice, and I know them, and they follow Me." – John 10:27*

> *Jesus said to him, "If I will that he remain till I come, what is that to you? You follow Me." – John 21:22*

The word follow may also be used to describe a choice as well as a command. Sheep follow the shepherd because he is the place of provision, affection, and safety. When Jesus told Peter to follow Him (John 21:22) it was both a command and an end to the discussion.

Regardless of how it is used, as invitation or command, when used by our Lord or in CHT, the opportunity to "follow" is never accompanied by force.

Yield

> *"But the wisdom that is from above is first pure, then peaceable, gentle, willing to yield, full of mercy and good fruits, without partiality and without hypocrisy." – James 3:!7*

The most common and often used request or command is to yield. To yield means to give way without resistance or bitterness. Every other command implies that the one receiving it will offer obedience and willingly yield; to come or follow without being pulled or dragged.

Yielding is a positive choice rather than the result of coercion. Yielding is not giving in, it is a willing response.

To yield is to comply, cooperate, permit, accept, or allow.

Go - Send

"So Jesus said to them again, "Peace to you! As the Father has sent Me, I also send you." – John 20:21

The command to 'Go' is either directional or used to establish action. One of the most difficult skills to teach a horse is a properly timed 'Go' - to move when you ask and not to move when you haven't asked. Some horses have a tough time standing still while others are so lazy, dull, or unwilling that riders have to ask, insist, ask again, threaten, then simply hope the horse will begin to move sometime before dark.

Giving a command to go, or to send, is a direction. Beating a horse away from you is NOT an example of a command to "Go!" but of dominance or rejection.

Until you establish a good "Go" you won't get very far with any other lesson.

I have yet to encounter any issue with a horse that is not the result of poor execution or an unwillingness to obey one of the basic commands: Come, Follow, Go, Yield.

TRANSFORMATIVE RELATIONSHIP

Christian Horse Training (CHT) is the process of creating transformative relationship between human and horse that produces faith strong enough to banish fear and mirrors the journey you share with Jesus Christ.

Many people who study horses and horse training have never had a meaningful relationship with a horse. Many people who study the Bible and Christianity have never experienced relationship with the object of the Bible – Jesus.

Throughout history most Christians did not have a book. Until the printing press was invented Bibles were hand copied and extremely rare. Yet there were many who journeyed with Christ. It is not necessary to read a book about a horse to enjoy relationship with one and no amount of studying delivers the essence of *horse* without meeting one.

One must have observed or experienced a transformative relationship to truly understand it. CHT speaks to the nature, pursuit, and experience of such relationship.

> *"Therefore, if anyone is in Christ, he is a new creation; old things have passed away; behold, all things have become new." – 2 Corinthians 5:17*

The epitome of transformative relationship is becoming a New Creation in Christ. The event that changes the old into the new is the arrival and home-coming of the Holy Spirit within a human.

Jesus was completely human. He lived a human life and died a human death. Yet He was completely divine. He is God. He is Spirit. He lives within every New Creation. Once the Spirit of God moves in, the extent of what is possible in relationship to God expands exponentially. It is truly limitless.

New Creations

New Creations in Christ are not the same as other people except for some personal difference of opinion about religion. What distinguishes New Creations isn't a *decision* for Christ, admitting the possibility that the Bible *may* be the inerrant and infallible Word of God; or even a fervent desire to lead a sinless life.

New Creations are, by definition, changed beings. What was is no more and what is born is radically altered from what it was because it is now *more* than what it was. A man transformed through relationship with Jesus Christ is not less than what he was - or the same *plus* a little – he is something more.

There is a change both seen and unseen in the newly

created being. There is an addition of spirit, a transformation of spirit, a change in vision, perception, and reception. When a human is reborn by God's Spirit the entire universe is transformed. An opening to God's kingdom and workplace cracks open; the New Creation sees more than he could before and knows more than he knew before. Limitations begin to dissolve as possibilities expand. New Creations look at even the most mundane things and events of each day differently from what they used to.

Every relationship you enjoy will not be transformative. Many people (and horses) will never know what it is to be changed both inside and outside by relationship. What is the practical application of transformative relationship for you as a Christian and horseman or horsewoman?

God made covenants with some but not with all. Yet the rain falls on both the just and the unjust. The ripples of history washed over those He chose and those not chosen. Every man must be respectful and gracious to every woman, but only one is his wife. Every woman is to be respectful and gracious to every man, but only one is her husband.

Children should be respectful and submissive to adults and those in authority but they only have one set of parents. You will not have a covenant relationship with every horse that spends time in your pasture or barn, but you are required to be a good and faithful steward of any horse in your care. Wouldn't it be wonderful if every interaction you had with human or critter left them with a net-positive result? Make things better. But if you can't improve something at least do not walk away leaving behind a net-negative.

> *"Spread love everywhere you go. Let no one ever come to you without leaving happier." – Mother Teresa*

Transformative relationships produce miracles: miracles of experience both tangible and spiritual. But the journey is not a series of ongoing miracles. Miracles are only miraculous because they are uncommon. Apart from Jesus Christ, the parties to all such relationships are ordinary – man, woman, or beast – but the result of being transformed elevates what is possible to an extraordinary level.

Glimpses and moments of the super-natural come, but they are fleeting gifts, not the substance of daily lives. Brief encounters with the miraculous and inspirational touch your life but can never *be* your life. The best moments shared with horse or Savior happen privately.

Transformative relationships are as unique as they are rare. Many people get a horse intending to create a great partnership but don't have enough commitment to finish. Likewise many come to Christ intending to complete their earthly journey in His presence. But, like seed that sprouts on stony soil, the heat and drought of life kill what began to grow.

Transformed by Relationship

New Creations are able to do things they could not do before. Eyes see more. Ears hear more. Worldview shifts. Fears begin to disappear. Power is received from God. The way such power is most widely displayed is through relationship - taking the gift of transformative relationship with Christ and replicating it in earthly form. This is the basis of discipleship with horses.

The journey of transformative relationship begins when new creations are born. From that moment learning begins, new faith is created, and it becomes possible for human eyes to glimpse what lies ahead and human ears to recognize the still small voice of God. The simple basics of some relationships between human and horse are similar to the essentials of relationship between God and man. Both are grounded in the truth of transformative relationship.

The difference between transformative relationship and all other relationships is that the principals are changed – they are transformed from what they were to something new, something more. Not only are the individuals changed, but the once clear line of separation has blurred.

In the process of transformative relationship total and complete independence is broken by one's own deliberate act. Transformative relationship binds two souls in a way no other contract, agreement, or partnership can. The more profound the transformation the more difficult it becomes to tell where one ends and the other begins or who picked up which habit or mannerism from the other.

The primary characteristic of transformative relationships is endless commitment. There is no deal breaker. The union is forever. Some may define forever as till death do them part while others believe that death has no power over the continuation of the relationship.

The experience of transformative relationship is not easily communicated. No one really knows what it is to be married until after the wedding. No one really knows what it is to become a parent until a child is born. No one truly knows the depth of bonding possible with a horse until it is experienced, and no one knows what it is to be one with Christ Jesus until he or she becomes a New Creation.

These events, a wedding, a birth, the recognition of a special horse, and the moment of rebirth in Christ are only beginnings. A new journey begins.

Fundamental Shift

The process of transformative relationship continues once the relationship is established. For Christians the process is called sanctification. Sanctification is the journey of joy shared with Christ from new birth until mortality becomes immortality.

Sanctification is the process of surrender and blending. Jesus never demands your will, your body, your money, or your future. He asks for everything and promises everything and more in return. What is promised? Joy, peace, provision, love, companionship, discernment, faith, fellowship, blessings and Eternal Life.

Transformative relationship may not immediately change the external appearance or circumstances. The change is spiritual. The change is emotional. The change is progressive.

A horse who is blessed by transformative relationship with a human may still live in the same stall as it did before accepting the offer of worthy leadership, but its spirit, emotions, and future have shifted dramatically. Horses in right relationship with a worthy leader are not anxious, aggressive, or angry. They are content, bold, curious, and secure.

Bo – my confident herd leader

Among all the people on earth this horse knows its master. What did that master promise? Joy, peace, provision, love, companionship, discernment, faith, fellowship, and blessing.

Eternal life may only be given by the One who alone can create life. There is no life other than that gifted by God. Humans can't give horses or anyone else eternal life. Christians know Who is capable of giving that gift to humans and horses don't need it. Horses never fell from grace or rejected God's plan in favor of their own.

New Creations in Christ don't automatically change addresses, jobs, or outward appearance. Pizza may still be their favorite food; liver may still taste terrible; and daily routines may or may not change drastically.

Horses in a transformative relationship with a human may still perform the same basic maneuvers or routines they did before, but the how and why has shifted. Obedience is a gift given because refusal has become unthinkable.

Relationship Habits

Two major relationship habits are of particular importance to the human – horse relationship.

1. Habit of Task, and

2. Habit of Obedience

The habits of task and obedience were first introduced in *Amazing Grays, Amazing Grace,* where my journey of discipleship with horses began, and are important elements of proper training and worthy leadership with a horse.

Habit of Task

Horses who learn a habit of task work patterns such as barrels and poles. Roping horses learn to position themselves on a steer and do it the same way run after run. Trail horses follow the horse in front of them. The easiest horses to ride are those who know their jobs so well that the skill of the rider is of moderate to little importance. Horses with the habit of task perform consistently with every partner.

Habit of Obedience

Horses with a habit of obedience perform behaviors or works as the practical result of relationship, faith, highly tuned communication, and commitment to the leader. The particular task or maneuver is of little importance. The goal of relationship is to enhance the bond between the equine and human, and obedience becomes a habit.

Horses, like people, may be taught to do repetitive work which is the basis of the Habit of Task. They do what they do what they do.

Reflexive obedience, delighting to do the will of the leader, is the result of blending personalities and spirits. It is the practical display of a Habit of Obedience that begins when transformative relationship is established. The characteristic that distinguishes reflexive obedience from what you normally expect is that it happens without thinking. It is an unconscious response.

Teach the Correct Habit

There is a danger in horses or people who survive based on the habit of task or depend on the quality of their works alone. Everything works well up to the moment when temptation, distraction, or danger enters the equation. When a horse is the leader and circumstances call for evasive action, the horse may bolt to safety without a thought for the person in the saddle.

The most important fact to a horse trained to the habit of task is WHAT it does. The most important element to a horse with a habit of obedience is WHO - the identity of the partner or leader and not the what, when, or how. When danger, temptation, or distraction arises the horse looks first to the leader rather than defaulting to the natural response of a prey animal. What matters is WHO is leading, not the particulars of the situation or circumstance.

Games and exercises create a conditioned response, increased vocabulary, or both. The natural language of horses is body language, making it the means by which communication begins.

A conditioned response is one of the simplest types of learned behaviors. The most famous case is that of Pavlov's dogs which learned to associate the sound of a metronome with food. A conditioned response is the learned response to a previously neutral stimulus. Clicker training is a type of conditioned response that may be familiar to you.

In horse training the sound of the clicker is associated with a food reward. Over time the horse learns to perform specific behaviors hoping for a treat but accepts the clicker as a reasonable substitute on occasion. The trainer must be sure to maintain the association between the clicker and food reward or the horse will eventually stop performing the behavior on command.

When the training goal is to elicit a specific response from the horse for each unique cue the horse builds a habit of task and builds a vocabulary making further communication easier. Trick horses are usually rewarded for specific behaviors with food or other substantive reward.

Transformative relationship also teaches routine as a foundation for building and expanding methods of communication between trainer and the equine partner. Games, exercises, and puzzles are the building-blocks of vocabulary in the same way words are in human language.

There is no one correct cue for asking a horse to walk, transition from one gait or speed to another, roll back, slide, engage a cow, jump, or for any other maneuver or specific physical response. There are two reasons why specific cues tend to be used by trainers;

1. Industry norms, and

2. Ease of connecting the cue to the correct physical response.

Unless you plan to be the only one who rides a particular horse it is good to teach your horse to respond to cues most riders are familiar with. Selling horses that have unusual cues is difficult and unfair to both horse and future partner.

One of my customers brought me a cute rose gray 3-year old Arab gelding for evaluation. She wanted me to figure out if the problem was the horse, her, or the combination of the two of them. The little guy had been in "professional" training for six months and his owner was still too scared to ride him anywhere except in a small round pen.

After a few days I gave her an update on the horse's progress. I found him to be a little pushy, but not in any serious way, and remarked that he had no idea of what "whoa" meant.

"Oh," she said, "He usually stops pretty well. The trainer taught him to stop when she tapped his shoulder with her right foot."

I admit I had never heard that one before. It was certainly original, but not helpful unless you want to purposefully train horses other folks can't ride. After sixty days the little guy went home with a happy owner and more conventional cues. Happy owners make for happy horses and happy trainers.

WHAT IS YOUR TRAINING GOAL?

There are two things to consider when it comes to training horses. First, are you trying to create a well-adjusted product for the marketplace? If so, then it's a good plan to know what the riders in a particular discipline expect in a mount and put those buttons on any horse you hope to sell into that market. Sometimes success is a conditioned response to a usual set of cues; the classic habit of task.

The second deals with the goal of creating a habit of obedience in your equine partner. CHT teaches horses the process of learning and a method of communication in order to explore what is possible through transformative relationship. The games and rules of an exercise only matter to the extent they build communication, confidence, faith, and a *delight to do thy will*.

Don't elevate any specific rules or steps to idol status. There are common foundations of all right relationships that never deviate just as there are fundamentals of Christianity that are not debatable. Before you can expect the Holy Spirit to interpret God's Word you must first open the Bible and read it. Before you can expect the inspiration to apply the principles of CHT you must know the principles of equine personality and behavior.

Christian Horse Training helps New Creations in Christ apply their own experience of transformative relationship with Jesus to the one they have with their horse. CHT also introduces people who love all things equine, and have already experienced the gift of transformative relationship with horses, to the same truth in God's Word. It works both ways because the foundations are built on one immutable truth.

The mechanisms of relationship differ in as many ways as there are relationships. The more I know about the spirit, fears, preferences, strengths, and weaknesses in my horse the less any particular set of rules or games matter. Something that motivates one horse may irritate the heck out of another. The deeper your relationship with your horse the more creative and efficient the process of communication becomes. Once a transformative relationship exists you move into the reward of relationship and the joy of the journey.

Most riders have a goal they work toward, whether dressage, mounted shooting, agility, or service work. CHT isn't based on riding your horse; it is concerned with loving your horse. The difference in CHT is that the primary reason to spend time with your horse is love. Training for a particular discipline is simply something you do together.

CHT is also the program most likely to re-balance horses unbalanced by genetics or experience. Abused, spoiled, or aggressive horses have the best chance at recovery in relationship with a leader who understands them, who meets them where they are, has the leadership tools and commitment to both make and keep the promises necessary to change fear into faith and hopelessness into security.

Success in abiding relationship with a horse is not a product of doctrine or any system marketed by a clinician. Success lies in the soul of the person who offers leadership to a horse and the equine who accepts. Listen to your horse with spirit ears and you will discover methods of communication you can neither explain nor market on a DVD. And in this you will be greatly blessed.

Do you Influence or Impact?

By definition, transformative relationships change *you*. Such relationships produce richer experiences and life events every day. They are deep. They make an **impact** in your life, your spirit, your future, and your today. Without them you would be someone else, not who you are.

Relationships have as many variations as there are coffees, espressos, and lattes. Some are thick, rich, textural, and deep while others are thin and milky to suit the palate of folks who really don't like coffee all that much.

Relationships require investment. Everyone has limited resources of time and energy to spend on initiating, maintaining, and improving relationships. Most relationships are like watered down de-caf coffee; you can go through a lot of it without much to show for your investment.

Most relationships today tend more toward the thin milky type. You may have many friends; the breadth of your acquaintance may be wide; but the relationships are shallow at best and only **influence** your life. But they do not change who you are.

Transformative relationships begin and continue with a significant, if not limitless, commitment. The quality of a marriage, a parent-child relationship, a horse and human relationship, and the spiritual relationship you enjoy with Jesus Christ requires a commitment of scarce resources, whether financial, energy, or time. It isn't possible to enjoy the journey of transformative relationship without making a huge time commitment.

Commitment to life-changing relationship is a choice. Do you seek to influence or impact? Do you seek a wide variety of relationships or a few that change your world?

I could step into a corral with 50 horses and influence their direction and speed of movement. Feeding and watering them for a week would influence their present well-being. But I can't make an impact on a whole herd of horses.

However, if I chose just one horse from that herd and bring it home I can change its life. It could change mine. The world would change just a bit because this new relationship began.

Do you think a herd of 50 horses really cares who delivers food and water as long as it arrives on a timely basis? I doubt it.

Do you think the one horse that came home to share the barn with me might begin to care whether I showed up or not? I think so.

Many relationships are shallow and of limited value. Transformative relationship is so personal that the soul is forever changed. Now that is **impact**.

It is Personal

Reflexive (unconscious) communication makes no sound. Nothing is more personal, more unique, and more enviable than spiritual communication with your Savior. The conversation between the human spirit and the Holy Spirit cannot be digitally enhanced. It is powered exclusively by commitment.

The beauty of transformative relationship with a horse is a parallel experience offered when you and your horse share not only a physical but a spiritual relationship. Humans cannot participate in the same type of relationship with each other because no one over the age of three can achieve the requisite simplicity that every horse enjoys.

What makes it possible for a woman to ride a horse without saddle or bridle at a walk, trot, gallop, spin, slide, and to *dance* as closely with a half-ton creature as any champion ballroom dancing couple? She only has to think what she wants to do and her horse carries her in reflexive obedience. Most people in the horse world will read this paragraph and immediately think of Stacy Westfall who rewrote the book on what is possible in relationship with a horse with her 2006 AQHA Congress bareback and bridleless freestyle reining performance in tribute to her late father.

[If you've never had the pleasure, or haven't seen Stacy's

performance with *Whizards Baby Doll* in a while you can easily find the video on Youtube.]

Have you ever had a conversation with someone who wouldn't - or couldn't - give you his or her complete attention? How did you feel, standing face to face with someone who responded to you verbally but kept looking over your shoulder for someone just a bit more important or interesting to speak with? Chances are this was not the beginning of a transformative relationship.

Have you ever done the same thing to someone else? What were you thinking? Most folks have been on both ends of that kind of drive-by experience. It is almost considered acceptable behavior today to converse with someone without missing a beat in your texting and tweeting, visits to Facebook, or checking email on your smart phone. Such behavior is ALMOST acceptable. But not quite – at least not yet.

Drive-by relationships are characterized by people who meet up with each other, slow down their feet or schedules barely long enough to make a quick connection, and then hurry off again in their original direction of travel. *So nice to see you, we'll just have to get together soon. Bye.*

Do you have a drive-by relationship with your horse?

Not too long ago I was busy with all manner of things at home and doing a bit of traveling for ministry programs. As a result I had not spent any significant time with my little gray mare Swizzle for three weeks.

Every day I was home I spoke with her and patted her as

she went into and out of her stall just as I did with our other five horses. But other than brief visits when I fed or picked her stall we had not spent any quality time together.

One morning while cleaning pasture mud from Swizzle's hooves I noticed that her feet needed to be trimmed. I led her to the door of the tack room and parked her outside. Many times I don't use a halter and rarely tie any of our horses. They are trimmed, groomed, vacuumed, and saddled in front of the tack room and I expect them to wait there patiently until we're finished.

Once I had my hoof stand, nippers, and rasp I was ready to go. I asked Swizzle to pick up her left front foot but she didn't immediately pop it up. Thinking nothing of it I asked a bit more firmly.

I got the first hoof into the stand and she left it there – for about thirty seconds. Then she started shifting around and pulled it away. It took a bit to get her foot up again, but I did and continued to work. For another thirty seconds.

For some reason Swizzle was being a bit contrary about picking up her feet and leaving them where I wanted them. Like all our horses, Swizzle knows that lightly squeezing the chestnut on a leg means *pick up this foot*. Swizzle is particularly quick to respond. Well, usually.

Swizzle wasn't being bad. She wasn't walking off or being disrespectful. She was just not being as good as she usually was and getting a bit sticky about picking up her feet. *How odd*, I thought. *What could be the problem?*

Remember how communication is often subtle and quiet? I

finally started listening to what Swizzle was trying to tell me.

"You haven't spent ANY time with me for three weeks yet somehow you think I should walk out here and be the perfect little pony anyway?"

Swizzle had a good point. I apologized and finished a rough cowboy trim on her front feet before walking her out front for a little hand grazing and finger-tip massage while she nibbled away.

The next day I did a full grooming job and played with Swizzle at liberty for twenty minutes or so. The day after that I gave Swizzle the spa treatment after sharing a quiet little ride together. Then I parked her in front of the tack room and finished trimming her feet. Not a whisper out of her and she stood like a happy little dapple-gray statue.

Swizzle reminded me that we do not have a drive-by relationship. She has been, and continues to be, both teacher, special-needs student, and a delightful gift from God. Transformative relationships begin and continue on the basis of commitment and time spent together.

COMMUNICATION

Communication is often loud, public, and intrusive. Communication can also be so subtle, so intimate, so personal and unique that observers are completely unaware of the constant thought and response between two spirits so finely tuned that they often "speak" with each other by reflex or touch alone.

The journey that leads to such intimate communication begins when both parties to the relationship begin to believe that in all the world *"there is none like thee"* (Jeremiah 10:6). None other can serve as a replacement. None other is as this special one.

Recognizing the inestimable value and complete uniqueness of one another is the first step of a dance that will eventually sway to music other ears cannot hear. The goal of transformative relationship is reflexive response; communication and movements that mirror and merge without conscious effort.

Transformative relationships are built on twin pillars of commitment and time spent in one other's company. People who don't want God to think that they're snubbing Him rationalize that investing NO time in His presence must somehow be better than investing too little. Certainly the intention to spend more time in the future must be more respectful than actually devoting too little time today. You have to wonder if such people believe they're really fooling God.

Do they think He hasn't figured out every last trick and deceit men can conceive? God Himself experienced what it is to be human. Jesus knows all there is to know about the content and reasoning of the hearts of men (Luke 16:15).

Do you multi-task when spending time in God's presence? Is there really something more important or interesting to do when you're in the presence of the Creator of the Universe? The three greatest threats to the quality of your walk with Christ are habit, temptation, and distraction. Multi-tasking may be evidence of all three.

What might God think if you allocate only a fraction of your attention to Him but expect Him to listen or speak to you? God may have a great deal to say to you, but unless you're listening with both ears there's little chance you'll hear one word.

How pleased would you be if you asked your horse to pay attention and he insisted on getting a bite to eat, checking out the neighbor's goats, and scratching you off the saddle because he has an itch? I doubt you would be thrilled.

Do you ever multi-task when you spend time with your horse? Is there really something more important or interesting to do at the moment? The three greatest threats to the quality of your relationship with your horse are habit, temptation, and distraction.

Building faith that banishes fear is a process of grace, experience, and practice. Time spent alone with God in His Word and in prayer is the foundation for faith strong enough to defeat fear. Faith grows every time God's promises are proven to be true. Every time tribulation comes and His promise of peace is found to be true, fear erodes.

Regardless of its actual history, every new horse arrives at your barn as a blank slate. Before you plan your training program or message you must first define your goal. Do you wish to influence the horse's direction or are you committed to making an impact in the life of the horse? Is this horse one of many or are you prepared to make a deeper commitment to relationship?

Your influence may allow others to see new possibilities, but making an impact in the life of another commits you to walk alongside him and experience new possibilities together.

One of the saddest – and most common – mistakes I see with horse owners/trainers is making a promise to a horse that they are unable or unwilling to keep. It is better to remain ignorant of transformative relationship than to be introduced to it, accept the promise, and then be discarded.

Keep your promises

Have I ever lied to a horse? Certainly. Lots of them. I didn't realize what I was doing most of the time. Sin is a lot like my training career; I made mistakes without intent and have been forgiven for them all. But once the Holy Spirit convicts you of error there are no more free passes.

Several times the Holy Spirit has as much as held my head softly between His hands so I had to look directly at Him while He looked directly at me. Each time the message was crystal clear about the matter of the moment:

You didn't realize that what you did was wrong. You are forgiven and the matter is forgotten. However, as of this moment you know that it is sin. Not only do you know that it is sin but you know that I know that you know.

God has a unique lesson plan for each of His children. What is not permissible for me may have nothing to do with someone else and vice versa. The purpose of this section is to open your eyes to an error you were unaware you have made.

The last horse I lied to was a big paint gelding. New clients sent him to me to fix. The gelding was also hugely talented with an extensive show record. But his last two relationships with humans soured him to the concepts of work, obedience, and trust.

The big beautiful gelding arrived spoiled, pushy, fearless, and dictatorial. After a previous visit to a trainer for a fix he had been allowed to revert to his bad habits which only made them worse. He was perfectly agreeable as long as he got to make the decisions.

Over the next couple of months I proved to the big guy that I was not afraid or angry at his threats. Lessons were prepared using the principles of CHT. Each step was so small that he didn't get a chance to offer a big refusal.

Together we built a habit of success.

The paint gelding had tons of ability but needed to correct some bad habits of frame and form. Before I could address performance issues I had to fix his problem of unwillingness. I "told" the paint gelding that I would never hurt him, that he could trust me with his life, and that he could believe everything I promised.

No matter what he tried the result was the same. I was fair. Obedience was easy. I respected him and helped him rediscover his place of strength and security that sent his weaknesses to the junk pile. No horse acts out from a place of strength, but from fear. I removed his fear by building his faith in me and in himself.

One day the big paint matched the commitment I had promised him. He said 'yes' to every request. He was delightful. He was pleasant. He was secure. He was happy. My clients were thrilled.

I sent him home.

I lied.

The events of the big paint gelding's life did not improve over the next few years. I don't know what eventually happened to him because I did not want to know. The teenager who rode him got busy doing other things and eventually became afraid of the big paint. When the owners called to see if I would fix him again in order to sell him I declined. I did not want the evidence of my broken promises looking at me every day.

I no longer accept other people's horses in training though I am thrilled to help whenever asked. I quit breeding horses because I did not intend to keep each new foal for life. I am acutely aware of what I promise. The Holy Spirit made it perfectly clear – He knows that I know that He knows that I know.

Do not make any promise you can't keep or don't intend to keep. The heart of Christian Horse Training is being worthy of your horse's faith.

CHT requires you to be honest with yourself as well as your horse. Is the foundation of relationship with your horse one that will last a lifetime or one that has a basis in achievement of some different goal? Transformative relationship is a solitary goal. There is an endless variety of ways to enjoy such relationship, but there are no equal or superior goals. It's you and your horse – and commitment without any deal breakers.

God expects us to be good and merciful stewards to all life within our care. He does not require us to offer transformative relationship to every pet or animal we meet. Before making any promises to your horse, decide which road you intend to walk and make the journey one of honesty and grace.

HOW TO BUILD (OR LOSE) FAITH

"Now faith is the substance of things hoped for, the evidence of things not seen." – Hebrews 11:1

"The saint never knows the joy of the Lord in spite of tribulation, but because of it." – Oswald Chambers

The purpose of obstacles is to transform hope into faith. Hope alone cannot withstand the trials of the world without first being transformed into faith. People who place their hope in the wrong things or wrong people are often crushed under the obstacles that roll or fall into their lives.

Obstacles appear in your life for one of two reasons, (1) to teach you to overcome, or (2) to redirect your feet. The greatest challenge on our place is Tire Mountain. It is only possible for horse and rider to reach the summit of Tire Mountain when smaller obstacles become nothing more than stepping stones. As a first step it would be too daunting for most, and failing to meet its challenge would destroy rather than increase faith.

God never asks us to do anything He does not first prepare us to do. God makes us able. The only way we learn the power of faith is to apply it. CHT uses the same process to build a horse's faith in our leadership.

Like CHT, your journey of sanctification begins at the beginning and progresses in an organized and predictable way. Which studies, exercises, and obstacles are milk and which are meat depend on your spiritual dentition, digestion, and strength.

"I fed you with milk and not with solid food; for until now you were not able to receive it" - 1 Corinthians 3:2

Growing in Faith – Trust in the power of the Spirit

The journey of faith continues until we are glorified in Christ or we quit. This applies to the newest member in the family of Christ as well as the one most senior. I learned this lesson recently when I saw the horse waiting for me in the round pen. No matter how mature in Christ we think we are there is still an endless opportunity for growth. No one is even close to maxing out what is possible.

When I schedule round pen clinics I tell the host I need three things; a round pen, a troubled horse, and an audience. It doesn't matter what the trouble is, a horse is a horse. At one of my first clinics I was introduced to a spoiled (fearless) horse. The expected group didn't show up so my audience was limited to the host, one minister, and two twenty-year old young people served by the ministry.

The round pen was far too large and I learned to limit the diameter of the pen. The second thing I realized was that some messages need proper foundations before sharing them. Because the horse was fearless the only way to earn his attention and begin a relationship was to introduce him to the concept of fear. There are times when soft hands of mercy need to become immovable walls of mercy.

Once I knew what I was up against I checked in with the kids to prepare them for what might come next. If they understood the respect (fear) we have for God I could use that to explain the context of the 'conversation' the horse and I were about to have. The next question I asked gets the same answer every time I ask it – except for this day.

I asked, "If you suddenly found yourself in heaven, standing in the presence of Almighty God on His jasper and carnelian throne, would you run over to Him, jump into His lap and yell, "Hi Daddy, what' sup?" To my surprise both kids said, "Heck, yeah!"

There went my chance at finding a usable context. I wasn't about to move forward with the horse because there wasn't chance one that the young people would understand. I decided to cut my losses, did a few other things then wrapped up the session. I felt like a failure, but did the only thing I knew how to do THAT DAY.

Just as I learned to use a smaller round pen I began telling folks who booked round pen clinics that I didn't care what problem the horse had – the more obvious the better – but I did not want to deal with a horse that was hopeless or a horse that was fearless. I have no problem working with such horses, but I believed that it takes so much time to reach a beginning of relationship that it makes for a poor program. Sessions are two hours long with a break in the middle for both horse and audience.

Because of the minimalist nature of CHT I didn't think I

could earn the focus of a hopeless or fearless horse and move forward into relationship properly within a two hour time constraint. For that reason I thought I had to set a limit on the type of horse that showed up for a clinic.

Either I was getting a little over confident or God thought it was time to step me up one notch in faith by sending me an obstacle – a big stout spoiled spotted mare. This was the first time I met a horse in the round pen I had seen before. I started to pray. If God placed me here He could handle the result. I asked the Holy Spirit to guide my feet and I walked into the pen – wired for sound – with a hundred pairs of eyes watching my every move.

I brought ground poles with me for the first time and used them. I was able to get the mare's focus and attention far more quickly and easily than I would have thought possible. I did what I had never done before in a clinic. Every horse I work with teaches me something. Bits and pieces from other horses and other days combined on this day through the mercy and grace of the Holy Spirit. What I thought might be a piece of meat too tough for me to chew miraculously became milk. Since that day I no longer limit what horses show up in round pen programs.

The obstacle came, was overcome, and became a blessing. Today there may be an obstacle you believe is too big, too heavy, or too daunting to face. One day God may place it directly in front of you with an audience watching your every move. Should that happen, have faith that He will also make you ABLE to overcome it.

The Process of Building Faith

The most miraculous result of relationship with Christ isn't that the circumstances of life that naturally lead to anxiety and fear are changed, but that *we* are changed so that our circumstance no longer triggers negative emotions. If your biggest issue is a nasty boss the Holy Spirit will not introduce Himself to you by swatting your boss into next week. He will enter in quietly and begin to change the way you see the world, your boss, and your future. The day may come when you feel sorry for your boss rather than angry.

Many seekers look for something more than their intellect tells them exists. Some pursue vices, some fame, some wealth, and some faith. Every Sunday thousands of seekers go to church for the first time. Whether they go a second depends on what message they hear and how it is delivered.

How effective do you think it would be to meet a first-timer at church who has a problem with alcohol by saying, "We're so happy to welcome you today. But excessive wine is a sin, so let's deal with your alcohol problem right now!"

Do you really think your visitor would return? Absolutely not. Your greeting proved that what he seeks will not be found in your church.

Making Problems Disappear

Horses come with problems just like people. Horse problems usually begin as people problems. Most trainers build their business on fixing horses, which is exactly how I got started. Perhaps a horse is cinchy, head shy, refuses to pick up its feet, or is terrified of water. Oddly enough many trainers introduce their leadership to the troubled horse by going directly for the girth, trying to pick up a foot, or turning a hose on the horse.

What are the odds that your church visitor will return if you hit him right in the bulls-eye of his biggest fear? What are the odds that horses will react any differently? Concentrating directly on the problem proves a lack of understanding, reinforces fear, and is a huge hindrance to establishing any relationship except a bad one.

The Holy Spirit changes people. Once faith is firmly in place old fears disappear. The same process applies in relationship with horses. The last thing I do when I meet and begin to work with a troubled horse is to address the symptom of his problem. The real trouble isn't the cinch, his feet, or water. The issue is fear. My job is to reduce fear by introducing faith.

When I prove to the horse that my promises are true, that I will not let anything hurt him, and that I will not ask him to do anything he cannot do, the cinch issue will disappear, feet will become feather-light, and the water hose will become a toy rather than a rattlesnake.

New Creations in Christ receive the gift of freedom from fear. Regardless of the circumstances they are able to say, "I'm good with that." The Apostle Paul was confident in good times and in peril. He knew His Savior and rejoiced in His promises (Acts 16: 25-28).

'For you did not receive the spirit of bondage again to fear, but you received the Spirit of adoption by whom we cry out, "Abba, Father." – Romans 8:15

The Holy Spirit is completely able to deal with any quirk of personality. Humans are humans and He is the most worthy Teacher. The goal of CHT is transformative relationship; the gift of freedom from fear to a horse regardless of any quirk of equine personality.

The process of CHT produces a foundation of faith between one horse and one person, not reliance on a particular saddle, cue, bridle, place, or set of maneuvers. Right relationship is undisturbed by circumstance, location, or time. Jesus' disciples followed the Son of God. They were committed regardless of circumstance, location, or time. That gift of faith and focus may only be given when it has first been received.

Faith is given to men and women as a gift of God. Faith is given to a horse as a gift from one who both knows and is known in return by God. Unlike the Holy Spirit, no human is guaranteed that his gift will be accepted because the process of our giving is subject to error.

The million dollar question is "How do you build faith?" The Holy Spirit gives faith as a gift to New Creations in Christ, but what process can you use to build your horse's faith in you?

The process of sanctification is similar to the process of earning your horse's trust – or anyone else's for that matter. Once the first requirement of transformative relationship is met – showing up – the journey begins.

A history of success is built by achieving success. Faith builds on promises kept.

Working with the Hopeless or Fearless

There is a lot of confusion over the character of God. Is He a God of love or the God of fear?

> *"For God so loved the world that He gave His only begotten Son, that whoever believes in Him should not perish but have everlasting life." – John 3:16*

> *"The fear of the* LORD *is the beginning of knowledge." – Proverbs 1:7*

> *"Do not avenge yourselves, but rather give place to wrath; for it is written, "Vengeance is Mine, I will repay," says the Lord." – Romans 12:19*

Over the years I have worked with hundreds of horses, including the hopeless and the fearless. Some horses think that people are pretty wonderful, offering affection, provision, and entertainment. Other horses think people are abusive, evil, and to be avoided whenever possible. Some horses are conflicted because their owners are not consistent.

God is the Master Trainer and the best example for people who wish to offer transformative relationship to horses. If you understand the role of love and fear in relationship to God you will become a much more worthy leader for horses. Faith is a product of relationship. Relationship is the progression of awareness, communication, commitment and consistency. It isn't possible to initiate relationship with a horse that is either hopeless or fearless. You must first introduce hope to the hopeless or fear to the fearless.

Hopeless Horses

Hopeless horses and humans have been beaten down by experience until they no longer acknowledge any possible outcome except a bad one. They have learned that nothing they do or fail to do will change their circumstances. Simply put, a hopeless soul has no hope. No hope of change. No hope of improvement.

What is the most rational response to this message, "No matter what you do or how hard you try you will never do enough or be good enough"? The only reasonable response is to quit trying.

If all I have to give won't satisfy your demand, what motivates me to give you anything at all? The pressure won't change; in your eyes I will still be guilty or fall short. If nothing I do will ever make something I didn't do right, why on earth would I keep trying to fix something I didn't break? Nothing I do will suffice, so what is my motivation to try?

If a horse is whipped because he moves he learns not to move.

If a horse is whipped because he stands still he learns not to stand still.

If the horse is whipped *whether moving or standing* he

learns to quit. The clear lesson is that there is no right answer and punishment will come no matter what he does. The hopeless horse does his best to check out of reality and simply wait for life to end.

Without the motivation to do anything other than wait for some sad end, those who are hopeless quit trying. They are done. Finished. No matter how much you whip or beat a totally defeated horse it will not move. Such abuse only proves that there is no hope. It isn't possible to begin a relationship with a horse until you first introduce the concept of hope.

Only the most able and committed people should work with hopeless horses. Each step is microscopic and requires the greatest balance between authority and humility, between movement and stillness.

Fearless Horses

Fearless horses are equally challenging. After twenty years working with stallions I appreciate the equine ego. Like humans, it can be both strong and delicate, and mask one emotion with some behavior that makes novices believe it is another. Fearless horses are usually spoiled horses.

Anyone without fear believes there is nothing to be afraid of. Fearless horses are very like spoiled children and spoiled Christians. They believe that no matter how great the threat or how loud the yelling, the owner, parent, or God will never actually hurt them. You've seen people threaten their horse with a whip, rope, or stick. The horse looks at the very expressive and usually frustrated human and considers whether or not he will condescend to obey. If he does the owner thinks he or she was masterful. The horse knows better. Why?

"You and which army, Bigshot?"

The horse knows from experience that if he ignores the antics and threats of the person there might be some noise, some dust, and some emotion – but there would be no real consequence for disobedience. The horse has no fear. Experience proves that threats have no real power. The choice about what will happen next is 100% the horse's. How many owners never figure it out?

Have you witnessed a mother running through this progression with a son who is doing something he shouldn't?

"Richard, stop it."

"Richard, I told you to stop it."

"Richard, I mean it."

"Richard, if you don't stop it…"

"Richard, I mean it."

"Richard, if you don't stop that this instant…"

"Richard, you had better stop or I will -------"

"Richard, I mean it."

Okay, you get the drift. Eventually mom quits and Richard's fearlessness is further reinforced. He is spoiled and he knows the power is his. Mom talks a good game but never scores a point. How many mothers fail to recognize what truly happened? This mom would make a lousy horse trainer.

Spoiled horses, children, and Christians are vulnerable. Their fearlessness is based on the lie that they have ultimate power and are immune from correction. They believe that no power can make them do what they don't want to do.

There is a deep hidden place of fear in every spoiled horse, kid, or Christian. Why? Because somewhere deep in their spirit they *know* they are not all that powerful. Horses can't command alfalfa to sprout from dry ground. Children can't acquire athletic ability or increase their height by the simple power of their will.

It may be true that Richard does have power over Mom. But he won't be under Mom's roof forever. A spoiled horse may have power over its present owner, but what if the owner sells it to someone else? Do any of you have the slightest doubt about who would win the test of power between a human and God?

I didn't think so. Christians may live without fear because we know our limitations – and we also know the One who has none.

It isn't possible to begin a meaningful relationship with a fearless horse until the concept of fear is introduced. There is no security in being spoiled. It is impossible to build a transformative relationship with a horse that believes his power exceeds yours.

Only the most able and committed trainer should attempt to instill the concept of fear into a spoiled horse. Each step is microscopic and requires the greatest balance between authority and humility, between movement and stillness. The goal is to create faith, not engage in a war of domination.

God – of love or wrath?

What about God? Is He love or fear? God is both ends of a continuum ranging from pure love on one end to pure wrath on the other - and every point in between. Hands of mercy sometimes erect *walls* of mercy.

Hopeless horses must meet soft hands that offer endless grace. Hope is reborn when love breaks through the scars of previous experience. Hope believes there is something more possible. It takes the most worthy, experienced, and committed leader to give the gift of hope to one who is hopeless.

God is the most worthy, experienced, and committed Leader possible. Not only did He create all there is but He will deliver on every promise made. God is hope and love in action. He is able to demonstrate love beyond anything we can comprehend.

Fearless horses sometimes need to come against an unyielding *wall* of mercy. Each block of foundation is laid so that it will never rock or give no matter how hard the horse tries to dislodge it. It is an immovable fact. Each time the horse tries to assert its power it meets a wall of mercy. Not discipline, not dominance – but something so certain, and grace so great, that it becomes possible to begin a new journey of transformative relationship.

God brings perfect love to the hopeless and displays unparalleled power to the fearless. From the moment hope dawns or fear cracks God begins to show grace or power in perfect measure. That same balance of need and provision describes the method and practice of Christian Horse Training. No one will ever match God's ability to heal or inspire, but He gives us His Word as our personal study guide and rule book.

God brings hope or fear for one purpose – to bring the one who receives His gift into relationship with Him. The only goal of CHT is right relationship.

Christians should be fearless – because the power of God has no limit.

Horses can become fearless – when they rest their faith in a most worthy leader.

Sooner or later humans will fail because we are not all powerful. However, the difference between those who practice the gospel principles of Christian Horse Training and other trainers, no matter how successful, is the source of authority and wisdom. Authority must be tempered by humility. Jesus is the perfect example. Wisdom is gained by practical experience in the round pen of life and learning at the feet of our own Master.

"In the New Testament, love is more a verb than a noun. It has more to do with acting than with feeling. The call to love is not so much a call to a certain state of feeling as it is to a quality of action."- Dr. R.C. Sproul

Love alone cannot drive out fear. Love alone does not produce faith. Faith is built upon a foundation of promises made and promises kept. Faith believes that the Master knows me better than I know myself.

People who aspire to be a worthy leader for their horses want to learn the actual process of building faith. How exactly do you do it and how does it work?

Building faith is a matter of experience and trust. Fear is far too strong to be driven away by anything less.

LYNN BABER

FAITH OVER FEAR – PRESSURE/RELEASE

Horses learn from the release of pressure, not the application of pressure. Humans are not that much different, we just have a broader range of options for communicating with one another. The natural language of horses is body language; physical changes that range from the barely imperceptible to explosive kicks, strikes, or bites. Extreme responses are the visual response of extreme emotions – usually fear.

Most folks experience fear frequently or routinely. Fear is evidence of a lack of faith in something or someone who is worthy of such faith. Christian peace is threatened by one of two fears; (1) Fear that God cannot handle the problem, or (2) Fear that God will not handle the problem the way you want Him to.

> *"My brethren, count it all joy when you fall into various trials, knowing that the testing of your faith produces patience. But let patience have its perfect work, that you may be perfect and complete, lacking nothing." – James 1:2-4*

Faith extinguishes fear. Faith grows each time a promise is made and kept; each time the leader is challenged and transforms an obstacle into a blessing. Faith is the result of having a master who *"knows me better than I know myself, who is closer than a friend, and who understands the remotest depths of my heart and is able to satisfy them fully, who has made me secure in the knowledge that he has met and solved all the doubts, uncertainties, and problems in my mind."*

Faith is built on a foundation of experience, not fantasy.

The initial brick in the foundation of faith is the first promise made and kept. Pressure is applied for only one reason; to teach a horse to seek the release. No matter what restriction or bind, horses that learn abiding faith become confident that every puzzle has an answer that may be found without any outside assistance. The horse learns to be curious, active, and how to find the place of perfect peace and release he knows is there.

The consistent application and withdrawal of appropriate pressure teaches a horse how to learn. The habit and history of success in finding the release steadily increases its faith in both the leader and in its own ability to discover the answer. As relationship proceeds the horse will begin to recognize small pressures as opportunities and information, not as restrictions or problems. He learns to persevere.

Not only will the proper use of rein, seat, and leg provide guidance and support, but the horse will learn to consider them as unemotional data. They represent input and are useful tools of communication.

Myth: Pressure is Punitive

Faith untested is little more than hope with either short or long odds. The cycle of pressure-release builds faith by comparing expectations with experience. Faith grows as each promise made is kept and each puzzle solved.

Some folks consider all horse training punitive. People with that philosophy believe that all pressure is by definition a bad or negative thing while positive reward systems allow each horse to decide what it will do -- if anything.

The only door to eternal life is relationship with Jesus Christ. The only opportunity for a domestic horse to be fearless and complete is through relationship with a worthy leader. Whatever God asks you to do He makes it possible for you to do well, even if it requires you to become something different or more than you were. Christian Horse Training seeks the same blessing between human and horse.

Faith Triumphs in Trouble

Several years ago my gray gelding Bo needed to stay in his stall when I turned the rest of his small herd out in the pasture for the night. As herd leader he found this a very troubling turn of events. Bo's dinner went into the feeder and he munched contentedly until he realized the other horses were heading out. Each stall measured 12 x 16 feet with a door opening to a covered 16 x 24 foot run. Each run had an eight-foot gate opening directly into the large pasture beyond.

Bo is a very balanced and secure personality. His status and performance as herd leader depends on the strength of our relationship. Until this event I had never seen Bo frantic about anything, but when the other horses left he started rampaging back and forth from stall through the pen to pasture gate and back again. He was about to literally bounce off the walls.

Bo has never doubted my promise to resolve all the troubles in his world. His job is to focus on me and watch over the herd in my absence. It was obvious Bo thought there was trouble. That made it imperative that I step in and re-balance Bo's world.

Bo had lost focus on me. His attention was running out in the pasture with his herd. I stepped into his stall to ask for his attention. The most fundamental command for those who enjoy transformational relationship is 'yield.'

When it comes to yielding, my horses have a foundation laid in stone. That habit makes it possible for me to regain their attention whenever needed. I needed to get Bo's attention. I use two basic exercises that cement this particular foundation in place; yield in reverse (back away) and yield the hindquarters. Both are accomplished by little more than body language.

I walked toward Bo's near hip as he whipped around the corner of his stall. I said, "Bo," and looked intently at his hindquarters. As if by magic – the magic of faith – he stopped forward movement, crossed his hind feet and yielded. Then he looked at me, took a deep breath, and dropped his head with a deep sigh.

Bo got a soft rub on the neck, a quick peck on the cheek, and I left him a minute later so he could eat his dinner in peace. Bo's anxiety evaporated the instant he gave me his attention. It did not return.

Bo crunched away contentedly while I sat down to consider what just happened. The power of faith firmly placed in me drove Bo's fear away. What a huge responsibility! Being a worthy master is a big job and you never get to clock out. No coffee breaks.

Not all horse owners aspire to transformative relationships with their horses. There's nothing wrong with that, but there is a minimal responsibility to be a good steward over any life or possession in your care, including animals. A till-death-do-us-part commitment isn't required for every horse-human relationship.

Furthermore, there is a commandment against false witness. In any relationship, horse or otherwise, do not make a promise you don't intend to keep. Don't offer a relationship if you aren't committed to do the work, spend the time, and shoulder the responsibility for all outcomes.

> *"Therefore, having been justified by faith, we have peace with God through our Lord Jesus Christ, through whom also we have access by faith into this grace in which we stand, and rejoice in hope of the glory of God. And not only that, but we also glory in tribulations, knowing that tribulation produces perseverance; and perseverance, character; and character, hope. Now hope does not disappoint, because the love of God has been poured out in our hearts by the Holy Spirit who was given to us." –* Romans 5:1-5

If God presented you with a tiny challenge that you lacked the faith or motivation to meet, why would you think the outcome might be different if He gave you some great challenge? Faith in God builds as you encounter bumps, obstacles, and perhaps a skinned knee along the road. Each time you face and overcome your fears by faith in God's power, the reality of what being a New Creation in Christ means grows into a much grander vision.

Christians are not immune from life's trials; Christians are undaunted by life's trials.

The step-by-step process of building faith using pressure and release - the habit and history of overcoming obstacles when training your horse - is covered in the Application Section toward the end of this book.

> *"If I have told you earthly things and*
> *you do not believe, how will you believe if I tell you*
> *heavenly things?" – John 3:12*

Faith vs Works

Which came first, the chicken or the egg? Does playing "games" with horses produce relationship or does relationship allow you and your horse to play together?

Most clinicians teach people how to get their horses to participate in "games" or ground exercises with them in order to establish control over the horse and begin to build relationship. The only proper purpose CHT recognizes for interaction and exercises with your horse is to promote focus and initiate relationship.

Games, exercises, maneuvers, skills, and all the *works* involved in horse training are the natural byproduct of relationship. Commitment is between horse and human, not to the acquisition of any particular skill set. Relationship is the beginning, the journey, and the purpose of a life lived with a horse.

> *"But someone will say, "You have faith, and I have works." Show me your faith without your works, and I will show you my faith by my works. But do you want to know, O foolish man, that faith without works is dead?" – James 2:18, 20*

Bronze trophies, big competition paychecks, high point awards, and championship titles are works. Most of you know successful champion equestrians who have demonstrated great works but ride horses who fear them or know their job so well they will perform it for anyone who knows how to ask. That person may say, "You may have a horse that will stand in front of a car to protect you from danger, but nothing of real material value to show for all the time you spent with it."

At the end of the day, when the barn is quiet and horses are tucked warmly into their stalls, is there love in the stable for the competitor with nothing but trophies to show for his work? I would rather share a cowshed with a horse that knows and loves me as a worthy master than to have all the bronze in Istanbul.

Remember Dickie, the horse who crawled under the fallen tree to obey his little girl? He had faith. Faith inspired him to drop to his knees to obey – a singular work for any horse. The little girl never won a trophy, but her faith inspired Dickie to works few others will ever perform.

"For without Me you can do nothing." – John 15:5

Transformative relationship creates a sum that exceeds the simple addition of both parts. A horse cannot jump an eight foot wall, nor can a man. Yet, when horse and rider work together it is possible. The current record for a straight vertical jump is 7 foot 10 inches. The record height with a sloping wall is 8 foot 1 inch. Together Puissance competitors are able to do what is impossible for a horse alone, a man alone, or for the majority of all horse and human partnerships.

FOCUS

God wants the same three things from me that I want from my horses:

- Show up
- Focus
- Offer obedience

None of the three concepts are complex. What Jesus meant when He told the disciples that one must come as a little child to enter the kingdom of heaven [Matthew 18:3] is that the entrance exam for heaven is too simple for most wise and prudent men to even grasp, much less master (Matthew 11:25).

Show Up

The opportunity to embark on the path to transformative relationship doesn't begin until two parties are present – they both have to show up.

The first step in either relationship is proximity. Someone had to create the occasion for horse or human to know that the trainer or Savior existed. The first of the three things I need from a horse is for it to show up.

Among the hundreds of horses I've worked with there

wasn't one that miraculously appeared in my round pen or barn. My horses were either born or adopted into our family. The circumstances of the birth of these little darlings were the result of my choice of mare and stallion, the actual timing of the breeding, and being present during foaling for most. Other horses came into my life and my barns when clients delivered them for training.

Those we adopted were selected from all the horses in the world. It was my choice of which horse was adopted and when. I noticed Bo, one of the amazing grays, when I saw his yearling photo on a Horses For Sale website. Bo didn't leave the ranch he was born on and walk into my life when he was two and a half years old - I walked into his.

After spending a little time with Bo I made the decision to bring him home. At the time I had no idea how important he would become to my own journey with Jesus Christ.

Five other horses share the barn with us besides Bo. Like Bo, Copper came to us as a long two year old when we saw him warming up in a round pen next to the parking lot before being sold at the AQHA World Sale in Oklahoma City. Our trailer was loaded and we were heading home but stopped for just a minute to watch the flashy dun in the pen. Copper returned to Texas with us. Copper didn't decide to hop into our trailer, the decision was ours.

I saw a video of Asti just before she turned three and bought her sight unseen. She passed a pre-purchase exam and was transported to Texas just months before Copper joined the family. Back in Missouri the black filly named Bubbles didn't decide she needed to move to Parker

County, Texas. I doubt she knew where Texas was. We were not surprised when this elegant young mare got out of the trailer in our barn parking lot. Every act and decision, every provision and payment made was ours. The process of adopting Asti was initiated and accomplished before she knew what was happening. Asti didn't establish the beginning of our relationship, we did.

Swizzle, Shiner, and Ace are all products of our breeding programs. God's grace kept Swizzle with us since birth and returned Ace and Shiner after a nine year absence. Again, Swizzle's birth and the rescue of the two Appy boys was not initiated by them. It was our action that led to the beginning or continuation of relationship with each of them.

Natural Horses and Worldly Men

Horses have lived in fear of man since the moment God opened the door of Noah's ark.

> *"And the fear of you and the dread of you shall be on every beast of the earth, on every bird of the air, on all that move on the earth, and on all the fish of the sea."*
> *– Genesis 9:2*

Horses are prey animals. They fear two-legged humans as well as four-legged predators. No self-respecting natural horse would choose to willingly walk into a round pen any more than a natural (worldly) man chooses to submit to Jesus Christ as Lord.

Once you bring a horse home the matter of showing up is

not completed once and for all. Each time you walk out to the pasture, paddock, field, or stable you expect your horse to show up. Day one is the beginning. Days two, three, and every day thereafter continue your journey of blessing.

For the horse, showing up begins the *dance* of relationship. Where the relationship goes from this first step depends entirely on the worthiness and commitment of the trainer (leader.) Once the natural horse learns to have faith in the power, the promise, and the constancy of the leader the transformation begins. What was once a prey animal will, through faith, become a bold, confident, and reflexively obedient partner and servant. The horse can become more than it was before.

Focus

The difference between transformative relationships and those that fall short is commitment to focus and obedience. Being able to recognize and direct focus is an important skill for horse trainers and magicians.

Wikipedia explains it this way:

> "***Misdirection*** *is perhaps the most important component of the art of sleight of hand. The magician choreographs his actions so that all spectators are likely to look where he or she wants them to. ... A phrase often used is "A larger action covers a smaller action." Care must be taken however to not make the larger action so big that it becomes suspect.* "

Timing and movement are tools used to engage the horse's attention. Rather than direct the horse's focus away from you, timing and movement allow you to attract it to you. Instead of the horse worrying about the llama next door, anxiety about being separated from its herdmates, or having absolutely no interest in you whatsoever, the creative (and sometimes artistic) use of movement and timing can draw the horse to you so it forgets everything else and concentrates exclusively on what you're doing.

Horses have the natural curiosity of animals whose survival depends on investigating their environment for hazards, food, or entertainment. Horses with healthy egos and normal responses are compelled to figure out problems or solve puzzles. What you do and when you do it engages the horse's curiosity reducing its urge to flee. Like successful magicians, care must be taken so actions are not so big that the horse's interest changes from inquisitiveness to fear; from *What are you doing?* to *Let me out of here!*

In case you haven't figured it out yet, many round pen transformations witnessed by audiences are tricks. The process of moving a horse from being untouched to being ridden takes more than two hours. In no way am I suggesting that the clinicians are anything less than skilled, worthy guys or gals with valuable lessons to teach to those who sit on the bleachers in awe and amazement.

However, these round pen transformations are very similar to watching a magician at work. Horses used in round pen demonstrations learn to properly respond to the specific body language, timing, and verbal cues of the clinician. I've done it myself, but it isn't a good illustration for the message I share today. The round pen programs I do now are based on calm, quiet, minimal requests that are easy and simple for the horse to do. My goal isn't to ride an untrained horse, but to demonstrate to the audience the basics of building faith that eliminates fear. I want them to see Christ.

Focus on the Giver not the Gift

Solomon, the wisest man to ever live, discovered the emptiness of seeking the gift instead of the Giver. Horses, children, dogs, and Christians alike are misguided when their focus centers on some treat, entertainment, bone, or blessing and not on the trainer, parent, master, or Savior.

The book of Ecclesiastes is avoided by many teachers and bible study groups because it is "too difficult." To put it in the simplest of terms, Solomon spent a great deal of money, time, ego, and energy on the pursuit of horse cookies. The conclusion he reached is that the pursuit of horse cookies eventually leads to an empty cookie bucket while pursuing relationship with the One who offers the cookies leads to eternal reward.

Every person has unique preferences when it comes to goodies, motivators, or stimulants. The same is true when comparing what totally distracts or tempts one person, yet can't draw the attention of another for two seconds. The promise of a new pair of shoes might motivate a teen age girl to do what her parents ask while that same offer wouldn't get her sister to come in from mucking the barn.

The things that provide motivation or meaning are not universal. What one horse considers punitive another thinks is great fun. Temptations are also unique to the situation at hand. What is a wonderful gift to one person may be the greatest of temptations to another. Things have no ultimate meaning or purpose and what is an opportunity to one for great success or joy may prove to be a stumbling block leading to someone else's failure.

Gifts, Rewards, and Transactions

Gifts are unidirectional. A gift is not a bribe, payment, or transaction and arrives with no strings attached. Gifts are presented and not earned. God provides every wonderful gift to His children because He loves us. There is no quid-pro-quo.

Bo, one of the amazing grays, is a full-fledged high order cookie monster. If a horse cookie crossed the barn in my pocket anytime in the past two days Bo smells it and will try and search out the present location of that cookie. Bo's concentration will be laser targeted on the scent trail of the cookie and nothing else.

I never use cookies as a reward for Bo. Part of my pre-work checklist is making sure my riding gloves aren't covered in cookie dust. If I ask Bo to show up and focus on me with the aroma of cookies present I have to work harder to earn his attention.

Actually, I don't use food rewards with any of my horses. They get cookies and carrots on a regular basis, but strictly as gifts – no strings attached and no behavior desired in return. When I am with my horses I want them to look at me, not at what is in my hand. True gifts are given without expectation. To do otherwise is to enter into a transaction, not bestow a gift or blessing.

There's nothing inherently wrong with using food as a motivator when training horses. The reason I don't include it in the relationship I have with my horses is that it tends to divert the horse's attention away from me. I want my horses to learn to look to me first. The best motivator is transformative relationship. Used improperly, food rewards can become temptations that turn an otherwise pleasant horse into an aggressive problem horse.

Many horses earn a living doing tricks to entertain audiences. If a horse learns to do tricks based on specific cues and the expectation of food rewards it is likely that the trainer could teach any number of other people to get the horse to behave in the same way; a trick in return for a cookie. But what wows the crowd is the trick.

God is the giver of all good gifts. Too many testimonies and evangelists preach the gift and not the Giver. Always make sure the preacher focuses squarely on the One who freely gives the gift and not the blessing itself.

Obedience that is offered simply because I ask is a gift my horses offer me. Performing a behavior or trick in order to get the cookie or carrot turns me into the third wheel. The relationship is between the horse and the gift, not the horse and the giver of gifts.

The greatest gifts aren't cookies, carrots, or other tangible items. The greatest gifts are relationship based; security, affection, provision, stimulation, responsiveness, and the conviction that among all others on earth, you are unique and irreplaceable.

Transformative relationship is seldom exciting and rarely entertaining to onlookers. However, to the parties so connected it is part of life itself and much of the reason for joy and happiness.

Focus on the Handler, not the Hand

Magicians want you to look away from their hands so you don't see how tricks are done. Christian Horse Training has a similar goal. The important elements of relationship are the parties in the relationship, not the accessories or tools used to accomplish any particular goal.

The Bible mentions many tools and assets of interest to those going to battle in His name like armor, wisdom, shields, ammunition, breastplates, chariots, spears, boots, and even soldiers. God has received requests throughout the centuries for each of these. But what is the most important thing to seek before marching off? Not any tool, but God Himself. God provides the means, the method, and the victory.

When training a horse there are plenty of tools and equipment hanging in the tack room. Nearly all trainers use saddles and boots, spurs and bridles, halters and lead ropes, as well as carrot sticks, clickers, cookies, and whips. When a horse is properly focused it doesn't think about any of these things; the horse's attention is on the hand of the leader - not what is in his or her hand.

Magicians want you to look at the big picture and watch

what they're doing. That is precisely what we want our horses to do. Don't make what you carry the center of attention. Teach your horse to share the moment with you, not zero in on the rope over your shoulder, a tarp on the fence, or the food treat in your pocket.

> *"Troubles nearly always make us look to God; His blessings are apt to make us look elsewhere." –*
> *Oswald Chambers*

It is imperative to fully appreciate the totality of difference between focus on a gift and on the giver; on a tool or the hand that holds it; on the provider and not on the provision.

Faith in an object has no power. Faith must be in some *one*. Your faith is in the power of Jesus Christ. The goal of Christian Horse Training is to build your horse's faith in your power to keep every promise you make him. The focus of relationship is never what you have in your hand, but what you have in your heart.

One of the greatest challenges you must overcome as a Christian is learning to look *past* a blessing in order to see God's face. Don't look at the gift, seek the Giver. It is equally important to help your horse learn to look for *you*, not for what you bring as a tool or reward.

TRAINING TOOLS AND STANDARDS

There are lots of tools used to train horses. There are hundreds of different bits and similar numbers of saddles, rein set ups, and all the variations in "training tack" that humans can dream up. From the German Martingale to a Running-W there is no end to the sometimes useful and sometimes tortuous devices hiding in the corner of tack rooms and trailers across the world.

Simply learning how to put on a particular bridle or restrictive strap contraption and how to pull on it does not necessarily mean someone knows how, when, and *if* to use it properly. Put a loaded automatic weapon in the small hands of a six year old boy and he can figure out how to shoot it by watching a cartoon or simple trial and error. Pulling the trigger is a far different skill from knowing how, when, and *if* to use the weapon properly.

Weapons do not belong in the hands of anyone who isn't trained to use them because someone might get hurt. Bits, spurs, and all the truly creative training paraphernalia do not belong in the hands of anyone who isn't trained to use them because someone might get hurt.

Did you learn how to apply a tourniquet in junior high first aid? They're not hard to make and come in real handy. But just because you learned how to use one doesn't mean you should go home and practice on your dog, little brother, or the neighbor kid.

CPR can save a life but it can also break ribs and cause damage when used on a person who is not in cardiac distress. Tools, tack, and techniques must be used only when they will benefit the horse. In order to use a tool properly –if at all – you must know **how** to use it, **when** to use it and most importantly know **why** you are using it.

The Hippocratic Oath requires physicians to "first do no harm." This is equally true for horse trainers. Have the right tools. Become an expert using your tools. Always err on the side of doing no harm even if it means you and Thunder only sit together and share a juicy red *aqql* until you are *able* to earn his focus and faith.

A Round Pen is a Tool

If you master the philosophy and application of round pen training you will be among the most elite trainers in the world and will be a worthy leader deserving of your horse's faith.

The proper tools make any job easier. This rule applies to horse training as well. Once you and the horse are in the same place the next goal is to apply your own uninterrupted focus to what the horse is telling you. Only then will you be able to quietly and methodically earn its focus.

A round pen is an excellent tool for establishing communication. Let's take a moment to consider the round pen as a tool.

Selecting a Round Pen

Round pens come in many designs and sizes. When establishing relationship with a horse I prefer a round pen about 40 feet in diameter. If the horse is aggressive I might stretch that to 45 feet. Anything larger and my feet will have to move far more than the horse's feet.

When everything goes well the horse's feet move a bit and mine move very little. My goal is to ask small precise questions or make simple easy requests. Running around is rarely evidence of success. I don't want to break a sweat and I don't want the horse to either.

Done well, Christian Horse Training is not good entertainment except for die hard leadership and relationship buffs because it moves forward at a fairly slow pace and raises little dust. In fact, the better my brain works the less the horse's body has to work. My purpose is to communicate a promise to a horse and prove that I will keep it. That is never accomplished by exhausting a horse.

Back in the earlier days of *round pen reasoning* clinicians believed that horses learned to properly focus when their lungs gave them no other choice except dropping from exhaustion. Can you imagine doing that today? Unfortunately, some people still think that a tired horse is a docile horse. Maybe for a moment, but once it airs up again you have another fight on your hands and you have proved to the horse that your intention is to dominate them, not to offer worthy leadership.

Round pens work because they are round. Recently I

visited a horse rescue to work with a couple of resident horses. The first horse couldn't be caught or touched. That meant that the first challenge was getting her to show up. I went into an area about 150 x 300 feet where she was wandering around hoping to attract the attention of a buddy in an adjacent paddock. A small round pen was set up on the other side of a gate in the middle of one of the shorter fence lines. After five minutes of *purposefully* looking at her from several positions she went into the round pen to where a bucket of feed waited.

The gate shut softly behind the mare and we left her to munch away in peace. I never initiate a conversation with a horse the moment I enter a round pen. It is only polite to let the horse have a moment to relax, nibble any interesting bits of grass, or investigate the round pen itself and the surrounding area. I do surprise a horse occasionally on purpose, but only when it is the right tool for the situation at hand.

Once the mare had time to recognize that she was in a small pen I went in to join her. The first order of business was evaluating how good of a tool the pen was going to be. Unfortunately it was only an approximation of a round pen.

The round pen was far too small and not round. The part of the fence with the gate made a deep corner. Horses are naturally drawn to gates as the avenue of escape and the fact that it was in a corner complicated things. Not only was I going to have to concentrate on what the mare was thinking I also had to defend the area in front of the gate so she wouldn't get caught in it. Corners make it possible for a horse to hide with its head in the corner making the hind feet the only part accessible to the trainer.

A dull saw makes cutting wood a bigger project than a nice sharp one. A hammer with a loose head makes driving a large nail into tough wood a real chore. Tightening a stripped screw is a lot more work than setting it with the right screwdriver blade in the first place. A properly sized and shaped round pen reduces the amount of time required to accomplish your goal and is far less work on both you and the horse.

Round pens should not have corners. That may seem like an obvious point, but most round pens simply are not round. It's easy to figure out why when you consider that most are made of panels or rails that are straight and not curved. This odd little pen was small, very oddly shaped, had a tree along one rail, and there was a corner that you could almost call a short alley leading to the gate.

Corners in a round pen are dangerous because they present a huge temptation to the horse. Horses are naturally drawn to gates and to corners. Horses can defend a corner far more easily than I can. They are also dangerous because it increases the level of pressure necessary to get a horse to move out of a corner once it has decided to defend it. Too much pressure and the horse could panic and try to climb out and over the fence. If you get too close when applying pressure to coax the horse out of the corner, you could be met with two hind feet in your face. Climbing over a fence is a good way for a horse to get injured and getting double-barreled with flying hooves can damage even the stoutest trainer.

The whole reason to be with the horse in the first place is to begin the process of relationship. Fighting a battle over who wins the corner is not a good beginning. When you don't have the best tools you may have to ask for less than you otherwise would or revise your original plan.

The amount of progress I was able to make with the mare was not what I hoped for. But, you have to adapt to every situation. The mare was there in the pen with me so we could tick the first goal off the list – she showed up. The next topic was focus. I wanted the mare to notice that I was there and then to believe that I had the power to influence her movement without making her anxious, angry, or aggressive. If I could calmly and consistently move her feet we would be gold. My final goal was to be able to run my hands all over her.

Have you noticed how difficult it is for some people to look you squarely in the eye? They recoil from meeting your gaze and may even be offended if you "stare" or pay too much direct attention to them. This mare did not want to focus on me. The owner of the rescue mentioned that she rarely looked directly at anyone.

Before the clouds opened up and we were deluged by a driving rain the mare not only looked at me but followed me with both eyes and ears, and even made the offer to approach me several times. All of us headed for the back forty to feed the herd there and I hoped to work with the mare one more time before the long drive home. Well, the horses got fed and we got soaked, but the weather didn't clear up before it was quitting time.

The rescue owner believes the mare did change after our time together, but I haven't seen her since. She's a beautiful horse with a problem but she seems willing to consider beginning a new relationship.

Round pens that are not round, are the wrong size, or have hazards anywhere in them place limits on how much you can ask the horse to move safely or may require you to move your own feet far too much. The winner is the one who controls the other's feet. If you're running around more than the horse is you are teaching the horse that he has far more control over your feet than you do over his.

It is wiser to limit interaction with the horse than lose ground before you lay the first foundation stone. How much faith would you have in God if the first time you met Him you had more power than He?

~

The moments when I feel the closest to sharing God's vision are when I am most disappointed by the level of response from one of my horses. What does God see when He looks at me? Many times I react to my horses the way I think God must react to my own behavior.

Why do I have to ask for you to focus on me? Haven't we already worked through this relationship basic?

I am asking you to come. You know I want you to come. You are able to come – yet your feet aren't moving and you look perfectly content. What's the deal with you today?

We're both wringing wet with sweat. I need a drink but I love you enough to get you one first. Here's a bucket of clean cool water. What? You don't want it? But you have to drink it or you might colic! What is wrong with you???

Why are you looking at me over the fence like you're starving and can't wait to come in and eat. Your dinner is in your feeder. The gate is open. All you have to do is walk six feet over to the opening and you can come in and chow down. Did you forget where the gate is? Do I have to come out there and lead you in? Seriously?

Why in the world are you acting afraid of the tractor in the neighbor's pasture? I'm standing right here and the tractor isn't moving. What happened to your faith in me that you should be anxious over a piece of parked farm equipment?

It's pouring and I just slogged out here in the mud to open the gate so you can come in to the nice warm and dry stall I've prepared for you – why won't you come in? I am getting soaked and you're just looking at me like an idiot.

Yesterday you did this exercise perfectly. Today you act like you've never heard of such a thing before. Who are you and what did you do with MY horse?

Every time one of these or some similar situation pops up I am reminded how often God must look at me and ask similar questions. Horses know why they do things. Humans can be far too complex and conflicted. Horses don't have to wonder, *why did I do that?* Not only do I have to ponder the question, but it's not always easy to ferret out the right answer. God always knows why I don't do as He asks.

When it comes to understanding the nature of humans, horses have us beat by a mile. Everyone knows that horses are far better people trainers than people are horse trainers. It's always been true and is still true today; horses do not lie to themselves or each other. Humans do. The worst thing about this element of human nature is that we don't always know when we're lying to ourselves! Horses are the perfect sounding board for working through what it is we truly think, believe, and intend by our words and actions.

Do you show up every day? Are you focused on your Master? Do you offer obedience reflexively or go blindly about your business when God is trying to speak with you?

What does your horse do – or not do – that causes you the most frustration or confusion? How might you be guilty of the same behavior in the eyes of your Master?

CHT ROUND PEN TRAINING

The first conversation between a horse and human frequently happens in a round pen.

Beginning round pen training is done at liberty 99% of the time, with no halter or rope on the horse. There are many ways to balance a horse, correct a canter issue, or introduce collection, etc. from the ground using a round pen. But you can't build on a foundation that doesn't exist, so your first goal is to get the horse to focus on YOU and not confuse this fundamental issue with the pressure of a bit, rein, cavesson, girth, or rope.

5 Unbreakable Rules

Five rules provide the framework and foundation for all successful horse training if you hope to inspire its willingness and elevate its ability through worthy leadership. These five rules apply every time you are in the company of your horse. We'll use an introduction to the round pen for illustration.

Only two things matter when you begin playing with your horse in the round pen; FOCUS and FEET. There are only two reasons why your horse doesn't do everything you ask; he is either unable or unwilling.

First Step in Round Pen Exercise - leave the horse alone

The first step toward gaining focus is to do NOTHING except get the horse into the round pen and pretend to ignore him. Horses I work with in clinics don't know I exist until after I observe them in a round pen first. Your horse already knows you, so just put him in the round pen, take off the halter and close the gate behind you as you exit.

Unbreakable Rule #1 - If your horse isn't calm and balanced do not move forward.

Let your horse nurdle around in the pen until he is calm. Some horses are traumatized by simply being in an unfamiliar round pen or by strange sights, sounds, or smells. Don't put your horse in a place you think will frighten him. It's fine if he's a little snorty or nervous, but it is not good leadership to dump your horse into a trap he thinks is life threatening.

Most horses tend to settle down after a few minutes in a round pen but a few horses get more nervous and hyped up the longer they are left alone. My promise to every horse is that there is no reason for anxiety, aggression, or anger when I am present. I have to climb out of a pretty deep hole if I let a horse get too worked up before we even get started. On occasion I have to step into the pen and immediately begin to direct the horse's feet to stave off a panic attack.

Once your horse is calm enter the round pen and, again, do nothing. Many horses think they have to start running around frantically the minute they enter a round pen. It takes a lot of time and great patience to convince a horse he doesn't have to run if that's the only experience he's ever had. I want the horse to calmly wonder, "Hmmm, wonder what she's doing here?" Curiosity is far better than fear or aggression.

Unbreakable Rule #2 – The instant your horse does what you ask QUIT asking. Know what you want before asking your horse to move.

How can I tell where the horse is focused?

Horses don't hide comic books inside their school books or mask their emotions. Since horses do not pretend it's easy to figure out what holds a horse's attention.

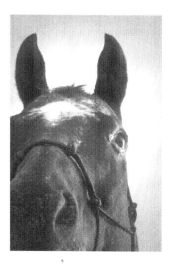

Where is your horse looking? Where are his ears directed? A horse's ears are like radar - always trained in the direction of greatest interest or importance. All you have to do is follow his eyes and ears to know what has his attention. Many times your horse will turn his ears in different directions. That's fine as long as one is turned toward you.

Your initial goal is to get one eye and one ear interested in you. Start small. Learn to read your horse and ask for very little at the beginning. You can ask for two eyes, the horse to face you, come, or answer more precise questions later. First… you need one eye and one ear. Do not try to KEEP his focus in the beginning. Your goal is simply to GET it.

Once I have the horse's focus I will ask him to move his feet. The instant the feet do as I ask I quit asking. Likewise, the moment the horse's attention leaves me my sole priority is to get it back. How do I get it back? By asking his feet to do something other than what they were doing at the precise moment his attention strayed.

When and how should I ask my horse to move his feet?

It is time to move your horse's feet when:

1. You lose his attention

2. He gives you the "pony finger", or

3. He stalls out and just looks at you as if to say, "Okay, so I'm looking at ya, whatcha gonna do now, Bigshot?"

In any of these three instances, ask your horse to move his feet in the opposite direction from where they were going the moment his ears left you, he gave you "attitude", or he dared you to come up with something new.

If your horse was moving left ask him to move right. If

you were bouncing a whip on the ground and he moves away keep bouncing until he stops. If he walked up to you when you told him to stay or stop, ask him to back up a step. If he backs up on his own, drive him forward. If you lose his attention while he is standing still and he gives you the "pony finger," send him out at a brisk trot.

Success secret: Only ask your horse to do something when you are 95% sure he will. You lose a ton of leadership credibility if you ask your horse to do something and he says, "No" and you can't fix it. Don't allow yourself to get into this pickle until you understand and are able to apply pressure where, when, and how needed to get your horse's feet moving in the direction you desire.

Unbreakable Rule #3 - If you aren't making progress or your horse is escalating in anger, fear, or frustration, STOP what you're doing and go back to a behavior you are 100% sure he will do correctly. Once you're back on the track to success move forward again using smaller steps.

In early lessons you won't push for more than one or two new responses. Know what your goal is before entering the round pen. Once you accomplish it - or fail miserably - QUIT.

Unbreakable Rule #4 - Most emotions except love do not belong in CHT sessions. The Holy Spirit speaks in a still small voice and so should you. You can't yell or beat a horse into faith and you can't work with a horse that is highly emotional. Love motivates your dedication to follow the rest of the unbreakable rules patiently and consistently.

Recap of Basic Rules of CHT -- Beginning Round Pen Behavior

1. Work at liberty without any tack or halter.

2. Know exactly what you hope to accomplish before entering the round pen; be prepared to change the program if your horse isn't responding as you hoped.

3. Begin every lesson with an unruffled horse.

4. Your only goal at this stage is FOCUS. Work to get one eye and one ear directed at you.

5. The moment you lose your horse's focus move his feet in the opposite way they were going when he broke his attention on you.

6. Know what movement you are asking for and QUIT asking the moment you get it.

7. Don't ask for something you aren't 95% sure you can get.

8. Always give the horse the benefit of your doubt.

9. Leadership promises freedom from anger, aggression, and anxiety. If you or your horse begins to get emotional it is YOUR responsibility to return everyone back to a calm peaceful state.

10. If you don't get the results you expect after several attempts, break the lesson down to MUCH smaller steps to guarantee that the next response will be "Yes."

The most difficult skill horse trainers must learn is knowing what to ask for and when to quit, which brings us to -

Unbreakable Rule #5 - Always end a lesson when your horse is happier and more confident than when you began. Every interaction with your horse should produce a net-positive experience.

Mustang Makeover and Misplaced Focus

Properly placed focus is always on the one with whom you enjoy relationship. The horse must focus on the leader and the leader must focus primarily on the horse and secondarily on his or her own Master. I never work a horse outside of the notice of my Superior. I am accountable to God for every move made and emotion generated.

The nature of fallen man is to focus on "I, me, mine." Anyone who sees the world through a lens of self interest is a poor prospect for transformative relationship. Eve ate of the fruit of the Tree of the Knowledge of Good and Evil because the serpent convinced her that the world revolved around her and not God. The first lie ever spoken was a doozy and Eve's self-centeredness bought it hook, line, and sinker.

The woman said, "The serpent deceived me, and I ate." – Genesis 3:13

The recent expansion in training and finding homes for formerly wild mustangs brings many new trainers to public attention. A recent program profiled a number of trainers on the road to one of the major mustang makeover competitions.

The first several trainers featured in the piece went to the auction to select the horses to which they would devote much of the following few months. I enjoyed watching these talented and invested men and women focus on the needs of the horse when making decisions about how and at what speed to offer new experiences or challenges. These worthy leaders focused on the needs of the horses in their care and not their own preferences, ego, or time-tables.

Then the whole direction of the program changed.

I didn't make it through the next story. I have no idea if the narrative made note of the drastic difference between the next trainer showcased and the ones before, because I quit watching. This trainer didn't want to pay the price necessary to select a mustang at auction so waited until he could pick up an extra one a dealer didn't want.

The criteria this man used to select his "partner" were flawed from the outset. He didn't seek a horse that spoke to his spirit or training style. Instead he picked the one he considered a cheap throwaway. He was motivated by his own ambition, not giving the horse a good start on a new life in captivity. His focus was totally self-directed.

The desire to compete or excel in any endeavor does not automatically disqualify a leader from worthiness. Many wonderful horsemen and horsewomen are successful in both the arena and relationship with their horses.

This particular trainer spoke with the words of a relational trainer but his behavior revealed the lie. He knew he needed the mare's attention. His method of getting her to focus on him involved a long line and a rope halter. The mare was very insecure and anxious and did not focus on the man. His method of "offering leadership" and gaining her attention involved pulling her head around forcibly to throw her off balance.

He pulled her around with brute strength again and again until the expected happened – she went over backwards from a full rearing position. She got up. He did it again. Over she went again. He was determined to get her attention using the only tool he had, domination. I do not know how that very sad episode ended because I quit watching.

This man couldn't see past "I, me mine." The poor mustang mare was nothing more than a tool to be used to prove his ability to make over a wild horse. His focus was on his own needs and desires. It would be surprising if he didn't have a similar problem in relationship with the Lord.

The Debate over Negative vs. Positive Rewards

Transformative relationships always focus on *who* and not *what*.

One particular online equine "expert" very kindly and decisively scolds anyone who uses any form of pressure and release when interacting with horses. Over a period of months he and I discussed a number of training issues in different horse-related forums. He believes that leadership is always punitive and the only acceptable method for creating a response in horses is the use of food rewards.

In other words, he believes that every method of interaction with horses other than food rewards is wrong. That exclusive belief is a significant enough philosophical difference to suggest that we might not find a meeting of the minds, but I believe his heart is in the right place so I worked through the process of exchanging ideas with him a number of times.

To no avail. I still run into him on a somewhat regular basis because of our mutual passion for horses and their welfare. However, the why and how of our methods may be light years apart. This gentleman views the horse as an animal disconnected from all others, including man. He reverences the horse and truly abhors any attempt to limit its options to remain separate and apart.

Food rewards can serve as a temporary means to capture a horse's attention. However, I don't want the horses I work with to see me as just a cookie bearer, I want the horses to know me, to trust me, and to hold a place for me in their 'herd' distinct and apart from any other being whether human, equine, or otherwise. *In all the world there is none like you.*

I've watched several of this gentleman's videos. In one he stands out in a pasture with a nice little mare that is quite attentive to him. She doesn't have a halter or rope keeping her there but she is obviously interested in whether or not he has a treat. She noses around while he's speaking to the camera about letting horses choose to be with you and not forcing them to show up.

A moment later he reaches into his pocket and the little mare gets her cookie. He continues to teach. Once that treat is gone she's back looking for more. His message requires others to adopt his method of getting a horse's focus using positive reinforcement and absolutely no pressure, or judges them to be in error and possibly abusive.

After one more cookie the gentleman shoos the mare away. Off she wanders to graze a bit. Then back she comes looking for another delicious little bite. I quit watching.

Is there anything wrong with using food rewards as positive reinforcement, aka **bribes**? Not at all - unless your goal with said horse is transformative relationship. Faith is not built on a foundation of bribery. When my horses see me come, which of these responses do you think I prefer?

"Here comes the guy with the cookies! Let's go see if he has one."

"Here comes Lynn. I hope she's coming for me!"

Do you see the difference? The first sentence is gift oriented. The second is giver oriented. I give my horses cookies roughly once a week, but there is no power or value assigned to the cookie. Horses that focus their attention on cookies aren't generally picky about who delivers them.

When food rewards are the foundation of relationship the sum total of the gift is the food item itself. The only value is the cookie, not the one who provided it. Send in the usual cookie provider empty-handed and a new guy with a cookie and see how long it takes for the usual gift-giver to be replaced in the affections of the horse. Be sure your watch has a second hand if you intend to time it.

Some people think of God as little more than a gift provider or blessing machine. They're happy to pay a little attention to Him as long as gifts arrive regularly. Stop the goodie train and these folks are liable to seek a new cookie connection.

Satan tries to lure us away from our Master and Lord by offering enticing cookies as bait. If he can keep our attention on the treat he can lead us away from the safety of the fold. One of the first lessons parents teach small children is to *never take candy from a stranger*. Children must learn to evaluate the giver before accepting what is offered as a gift.

When relationship with God is based on the value of gifts there is no place for faith. When tribulation comes, and it will [John 16:33], the believer who seeks the gift and not the Giver has nothing to stand on, to shelter under, or to cling to.

Horses conditioned to respond to food rewards have nothing to rely upon when frightened except the fear God instilled in them in Genesis 9. Without faith the vacuum is filled with fear. These horses learn that man offers nothing more valuable than cookies. Do you really think that the terrified horse you're riding as it bolts for the hills will hit the brakes if you manage to reach over his sweaty outstretched neck and offer him a cookie?

Something that is unearned is either a gift or an entitlement. One learns by experience that the gift will arrive without any effort on his part. Over time, regularly delivered unearned gifts are no longer considered a blessing but a right. Instead of something extra it becomes something due and payable. In times of social crisis looting and destruction occur when people do not get what they think is their due. They revolt.

Well adjusted people and animals appreciate what is provided for them. Things often get ugly when gratitude turns into entitlement. Horses with food aggressions demand what they think is rightfully theirs but at the same time are fearful. Such horses focus on the food bucket, not on the hands that deliver it to the paddock or stall.

God knows that we cannot focus on Him if our daily needs are not met. Animals in the wild don't play, nap, or seek relationship with others until the basic need for food and water is satisfied. Pasture horses work up to sixteen hours a day taking care of the basics. That doesn't leave a lot of free time to get into trouble or contemplate a social calendar.

Copper and Swizzle "working"

Domestic animals expect all their basic needs to be met. Time is available to focus on the giver because they don't have to burn much daylight worrying about the simple things of life. Such freedom offers a great opportunity to engage in relationship as well as a whole lot of free time to get into mischief. The easiest way to keep people, horses, and dogs content and productive is the right balance of work, play, and rest. Too little work or productive play and there's no telling what trouble they'll get into with all the free time and excess energy available.

There is no blessing in a relationship that only lasts as long as the treats hold out. The horse doesn't make a commitment of relationship to the deliverer of gifts because he or she has little or no unique identity or personal value. Do you imagine God is pleased with people who don't care about who He is but only what He provides?

Relationships based on bribery can last quite a while, even if the recipient doesn't get a cookie each and every time the gift giver shows up. But the strength of the positive association begins to decay when not reinforced with more bribes and will eventually extinguish altogether if the gifts stop coming.

There is a time and place for using food as a reward when training horses and dogs – and people. Some folks believe you should use rewards to build relationship. The emphasis is placed on the object being offered as an incentive to show up or learn a particular trick.

My mother wrote in my baby book that I sang myself to sleep at age two or three with the Doxology. She obviously thought it noteworthy though later entries documented my complete inability to carry a tune. I don't remember doing it, but am not surprised considering the lyrics.

> *Praise God from whom all blessings flow,*
> *Praise Him all creatures here below.*
> *Praise Him above ye heavenly hosts,*
> *Praise Father, Son, and Holy Ghost.*

Even a child understands the simplicity of worship in the Doxology. And, as an animal nut from birth, I felt more at home in the wonderful company of *all creatures here below* who praised the One who made them than I did with my human companions.

All blessings come from God. May we humans learn to be as simple and wise as *all creatures here below* by seeking the Giver and not the gift.

Confusing Tools and Gifts

Wisdom is a gift. Discernment is the prize of each hard won battle over the world and the flesh. Distinguishing between a tool and a gift can be a bit challenging sometimes. How does this fact affect your walk with Christ and your ability to be a worthy leader and horse master? Here's an illustration to get you thinking.

If a husband gives his wife a vacuum cleaner for their first wedding anniversary will she be pleased or disappointed? Is the vacuum a gift or a tool disguised as a gift?

The answer depends completely on the wife. She may have had her eye on that power-beating rug-sucking cleaner for a long time and is thrilled with the opportunity to start the engine on her very own unit. Or, she may look at the vacuum as a thinly-veiled criticism from a husband who is more like Felix Unger than Fabio. It adds injury to insult to insinuate that the bride is a poor housekeeper giving her a tool instead of something more romantic. Tying up a package of Hoover and chocolate-covered strawberries with the same bow may not generate the response her husband seeks. Unless, of course, he never wants to see anniversary number two.

Gifts of the Spirit are not gifts in the same sense as birthday or anniversary gifts. They are unearned and unmerited. Spiritual gifts are not transactions, but they are not given without some expectation from the recipient.

I can't remember a time in my life when I wasn't trying to accomplish some goal. Whether caring for in-laws with failing health or working to make my business profitable, the times of doing just what I wanted to do have been few and far between. Certainly I made the choice to be self-employed and care for family members, but I had very few hours to fill completely as I wished. Not surprisingly I love horses and working with them. The years I spent in the horse business were *years spent in business*, not years spent playing with my own horses.

Four years after God put me to work exclusively for Him I had a knee replaced which made it possible for me to get back in the saddle for more than the short quiet rides of recent years. The temptation to devote all my time to working with my own horses, caring for our place, and enjoying these golden years with my husband here in our cozy barn has crossed my mind several times.

Just how important is the work I do for the ministry? God has so many people carrying His messages that have far larger audiences than I do. Is it really important for me to keep putting in the hours of study, writing, and trying to impact the life of other folks and their horses? I'm just a nobody living in Weatherford, Texas. Maybe this gift of renewed physical ability is one I can open and enjoy for the time left. Who would notice if I quit trying to be heard by anyone other than my own horses? Why shouldn't I simply retire and enjoy all that God has provided?

The more time I spend improving my balance and fitness, working with my horses, and the higher I raise the bar of what is possible in relationship with them the more fulfilling, satisfying, and FUN it becomes. The remnants of adrenalin and ambition, competition, accomplishment, and self-satisfaction from my training days still get stirred up from time to time.

During my years in the horse industry my life was horses – 100% horses. Training, breeding, judging, marketing, showing, sales, and keeping up with ever-expanding facilities took all my time and more. Everything I did was directly tied to what I did – horses. Only later, when I retired due to physical incapacity did God reveal that everything in my life to date was simply preparation for the *rest* of my life.

Have you noticed that the word *retirement* is not in the Bible?

The living we earned in past years allows us to enjoy our horses so far without worrying overmuch about how the feed bill will be paid. While drinking a cup of coffee on the barn porch recently I ruminated about whether or not I was truly taking advantage of the wonderful gifts God had given me. This message came:

"I gave you great gifts to use in service for Me."

Dogs sprawled at my feet as five frolicking soon-to-be-weaned doelings played a few yards away in the gauzy sunlight of early morning as this question presented itself:

"Why do we train horses and educate children?"

The purpose of education and training is to create utility – tools, if you will, for future use. Training horses properly should be a gift of sorts to them and education is a gift to children and adults alike. Training and education prepares the student to reach his or her potential and be productive or of great service to others.

"Why does God give us great gifts?"

For reasons He alone knows, God blesses us with His Spirit and worldly experience in order to enhance the relationship we have *with* Him and to make us more useful *to* Him. God prepares us for Himself - and for His purpose in service to others in the family of Christ. All the gifts and blessings God has bestowed upon me are for my benefit and joy as well as tools to use in His employ.

Gifts received from God are not to be the center of interest or object of our attention. What they are intended to do is point the way to the face of the Giver. They are not horse cookies to be consumed and forgotten. Did God give me a new knee and the ability to pursue my passion for horses for no other purpose than to enjoy it? Has He gifted me with insight and access to His Word for my edification alone?

Probably not, but is it worth all my time trying to get the message right? Am I wasting His gifts by spending so much time in my office while six horses wait for me to show up on their side of the barn?

God has blessed me beyond expectation and far beyond what I deserve. Sometimes God gives His blessings less like horse cookies and more like vacuum cleaners. What He provides is given to be used in His service. God never forces us to comply, but when you delight to do His will there really is no other option.

Every time I am tempted to quit doing His business and enjoy retirement I realize that I am already doing what I want to do. My journey is one of joy. The option to indulge myself in the luxury of an undeserved gift can be tempting and may indeed be a direct assault from the evil one, but no sooner does such a thought cross my mind than peace descends once more in the sure knowledge that I would have it no other way. There is nothing I would rather be than a tool in God's tool box, available and ready whenever He reaches in.

The same is true for horses in right relationship with a worthy master. Blessings given draw your horse's focus to you and not to the cookie. CHT is the process of building transformative relationship so the horse seeks to be the tool you prepare him to be. Not only are you separate from all others on earth, but your horse is doing what he wants by doing what you want.

God will never ask you to do something He has not made you able to do. No worthy leader will ask a horse to do something he has not been prepared to do. God makes able; your bit is to be willing. You make your horse able and by the gift of relationship he will not only be willing, but will delight in the doing.

LEAVING GOD'S GIFTS UNOPENED

One summer morning the local meteorologist forecasted a high of 105 degrees. I had planned to spend lots of time with the horses, but 105 degrees is too hot to do much – for them or me. In order to salvage any part of the day with my ponies I took a cup of coffee outside and sat in a plastic chair on a patch of grass where Bo and Copper grazed.

Being busy in the Lord's work is a far different animal from being TOO busy doing the Lord's work. One is a great gift and the other an error. Lately I was running short on horse time and long on time spent at my computer, trying to get the next manuscript ready and keep up with social media. So this morning I went out as soon as the basic morning chores were complete.

For what was supposed to be a scorching day the morning offered an unexpected and delightfully cool breeze. I closed my eyes and basked in the moment while horses nurdled beside me. Shade. Quiet. Cool. Breezy. Bliss.

Then temptation wormed into my perfect moment. I was struck with a pang of guilt when I remembered that I had not done my morning study yet. I had put this time alone with the horses before time alone with God and His Word. Can you guess my next thought?

Get thee behind me, Satan.

Seriously, that was my next thought. What better opportunity to enjoy the gift of God and time alone with Him than right where I was? What better opportunity could there be to praise God than here in the cool shade of the morning with *all creatures here below*?

As if on cue, Bo and Copper ambled over to my chair for a scratch and to nibble the grass between my feet. In the beauty of the morning God presented me with a front row seat to the gift of delight in His creation and the amazing meteorological performance of the day so far.

God delivers gifts every day that are never opened. All His gifts are based on simplicity and peace. Did Jesus ever scurry to a new destination or rush a meeting with His disciples? God's message is joy, serenity, and faith. Complexity and busyness are the invention of man, not horses and not God.

Another gift from God.

How many times have you run past a gift because you were too busy to notice? I couldn't count the times I've been guilty. What are you too busy doing? Something for God or something disguised as work that is really a temptation intended to divert your attention from the Giver to the gift?

Gift or Giver, Transaction or Transformation

For something to be the truth it must be true in every situation and in every time. The pitfalls of focusing on the gift rather than the Giver are true and generalize well. The author of a popular book on working with wild horses realized this truth but failed to see it for what it was.

She wrote that horses do what she asked because she pays them with a click and a treat. Horses are happy when they earn the food reward. Many like-minded horse owners consider her a shining example and follow her methods.

The relationship this author endorses with horses is **transactional** in nature and is described as a "contract" with horses. If you perform for a paycheck you don't really care who signs it. Your main concern is that it arrives on time and doesn't bounce. Payment for obedience is a business deal, not a relationship.

What conclusions did the author reach?

- The author expressed regret when she actually did establish leadership with a horse because it required far more maintenance than just giving a treat in exchange for desired behavior. In other words, there is far greater commitment required to build relationship than teach a trick. She is right.

- Like people, horses who expect to be paid on time complain when they don't get what they believe they are owed. When confronted by a biting horse the author resolved the problem by giving it the treat. There is a basic truth of nature that you get more of what you reward. Rather than correcting or disciplining the horse that learned to bite it was rewarded for being aggressive. Guess what lesson the horse really learned?

- The author also discovered that clickers and treats do not balance a horse that is already unbalanced. I agree whole-heartedly.

- Throughout the process of using positive rewards (clickers and treats) horses that begin with anger or aggression issues (pushy and demanding) tend to retain those issues. The horses offer whatever behavior they believe should earn the treat and act out in aggressive ways when payment isn't delivered.

The most interesting discovery the author shared is how perceptive horses can be. When she went out to play with the horses without wearing the expected clothing that carried a supply of treats the horses refused to participate. No paycheck, no work. Smart horses.

Leadership by temptation or bribery is not leadership. It is a business deal.

The Personal Nature of Gift Giving

The value of many gifts depends entirely on the identity of the giver. Business transactions depend on both sides getting what they expect from the deal. Do you care which bank employee processes your mortgage payment when the check clears your account? When you order a book on Amazon do you care who packs it for shipment? If a horse expects a food reward when he hits his mark or completes a behavior does he really care who gives him the treat?

A dress has no interest in who wears it and a car does not recognize one driver over another. A diamond may be the solitaire set in a wedding band or the jewel in a belly dancer's navel. Makeup doesn't care whose hand applies it and a putter could care less about the owner of the golf bag.

Whether the item is an engagement ring or a wildflower bouquet, the importance of the gesture depends on who offers it.

From an early age parents teach their children not to accept candy or gifts from strangers. It is not unusual for two people to offer a horse a carrot with one being happily crunched and the other refused. The carrot accepted was in the hand of the person with whom the horse enjoyed transformative relationship. The other carrot was in the hand of a stranger.

Blue, my elderly Australian Shepherd, loves dog cookies but will seldom take a cookie from a stranger. Blue has been going to one veterinarian office since he was a tiny puppy. The people at the clinic are wonderful and love him.

When they try to give him a bone he eventually takes it, only to drop it on the floor. The same thing happens at the groomer. Blue gets clipped regularly to keep him cool and comfortable. When pressed he will accept a treat – and drop it on the ground. If I pick it up and offer it he chows it right down. Blue is totally fixated on the giver.

Do you evaluate the giver based on the gift or the gift based on the giver?

REFLEXIVE OBEDIENCE

"I delight to do Your will, O my God, and Your law is within my heart." – Psalm 40:8

The fundamental shift isn't always *what* a New Creation in Christ does, but *how* and *why* things are done. When our Savior calls there is no "Why?" -- there is only "Yes."

There is a significant difference between "Thy will be done" (Luke 11:2) and "I delight to do Thy will." The former may indicate a preference for a different path but submits to the will of the Master. In other instances "Thy will be done" may be the simple recognition that nothing in the world happens unless the Creator of the Universe decrees or permits it.

The latter, "I delight to do Thy will," is personal and recognizes no Option B; there is only delight in doing, being, and relating to the Master. There *is none but Thee* and *Thy will is my will*. It is simple, profound, and transformative.

New Creations are extensions of Christ through the indwelling of His Holy Spirit. As sanctification proceeds His will becomes your will and His vision your vision.

The goal of a New Creation (or horse) in transformative relationship is communion with the Master. The purpose is to rest beside the Master, move as directed, be spontaneously obedient, and in every circumstance look first to Him. Regardless of what eyes see, ears hear, or spirit perceives – focus moves without thought to the Master – first, always, and only. Unless you obey in the present moment God cannot share what comes next.

All of God's revealed truths are sealed until opened through obedience. You will never open them through philosophy or thinking. Let God's truth work by immersing yourself in it, not by worrying into it. The only way you can get to know the truth of God is to stop trying to ferret it out and be born again. If you obey God in the first thing, He moves seamlessly on to the next.

Trail courses are designed in a particular order. The only way to correctly advance from one obstacle to the next is to follow the plan. Competitors in any trail or obstacle class present each challenge to the horse in order and only ride one at a time. The surest way to mess up an obstacle course or reining pattern is to think ahead and stop concentrating on the present puzzle.

Years ago in Florida I judged a 57 horse trail class with several other judges. Trail was one of 100-plus more classes we judged and the afternoon was warm and sunny. Another judge and I sat in chairs close to the ninth or tenth obstacle. More than halfway through the class the judge next to me said, "How did that rider get there?"

The competitor was negotiating a box/ground rail

combination about ten feet away from where we sat. My colleague had fallen asleep in the sun for a moment and was disoriented for a split second when he awoke. When he asked how the rider got to the obstacle I replied, "The usual way." I don't know how he scored the run but at least he knew the rider rode the pattern correctly.

Cross-country Course of Life in Christ

There are only two ways to ride a horse: (1) You ride *some thing*, an immediate puzzle or obstacle, or you (2) ride the horse *somewhere*. Riding a puzzle draws your focus to the specific placement of each of your horse's feet and each part of his body. The other way is to ride toward a destination in the distance. Riding *some where* directs your eyes and intention well ahead of your horse's body. You will reach your destination sooner or later as long as your horse goes where your eyes look.

Cross-country jumping competitions are an interesting mix of the two. Horse and rider gallop forward until a jump or obstacle presents itself. The rider prepares the horse, flies over or through the obstacle, and then extends stride, focus, and attention as the horse gallops across the countryside to the next challenge.

The goal of cross country jumping is to negotiate a clear round with no disobediences, falls, or errors. Life is like a cross-country competition. It must be lived according to God's design and only those with perfect scores may cross the finish line. Perfection is only achieved when Jesus accompanies us during the ride.

Offer Obedience

Much has been written within the Christian community about obedience. Some pastors, scholars, and writers opine that God's primary desire is for our obedience, implying that obedience is the fundamental issue of relationship with Him. Many horse trainers also believe that the purpose of lessons, correction, discipline, and practice is to elicit obedience from the horse.

Yes – and no.

The most important relationship you have is with Jesus Christ. Obedience is certainly on the list of what God expects from us, but it isn't the first item on the list.

Obedience isn't the heart of chosen relationships; obedience is the fruit of such relationship.

Do you consider whether or not you will obey Jesus on a daily basis? Hourly? By the minute?

Once your commitment is made the moments of conscious decision about whether or how to obey become less frequent. In the beginning days of transformative relationship many elements or habits of the "old man" must be considered and confirmed, rejected, or remodeled. [Romans 6:6]

What does this new relationship with Jesus mean to all your existing friendships and associations? How does it impact the way you spend your time? Does it affect what you eat, your recreational pursuits, and how you look at the people and world around you?

As relationships deepen obedience becomes more reflexive. It becomes increasingly automatic and unconscious. Eventually you won't even think about obeying the Lord – you simply do.

Reflexive Obedience

Reflexive obedience is as automatic as breathing. The autonomic nervous system controls physical necessities like breathing, heartbeat, blood pressure, digestion and sweating. Respiration happens without conscious management. Your heart beats whether you ask it to or not. The popcorn you had last night digested while you slept. After a long day on the trail your horse may be a sweaty mess. He didn't sweat because he decided he wanted to sweat; it happened because it was the right thing for his body to do to keep critical systems interacting properly.

Sometimes we are acutely aware of our breathing or heartbeat. This usually happens in times of imbalance or illness. The medical system provides treatment and support when the automatic relationships in your body don't work as they were intended to. Optimum health describes the condition where all of the bodily systems and relationships work together without conscious effort or intervention.

That describes reflexive obedience pretty well. There are probably dozens of examples every day where you are reflexively obedient to God. You can't write them down in a list because they happened automatically – He never made a specific request and you didn't have to make a decision about whether or not to obey.

As a New Creation in Christ you are different; something more than what you were. Your spirit is now more than mortal because of the indwelling Spirit of God. Many of your actions are the result of this real mortal-immortal spirit, not simple conscious obedience to a Master.

Think about something that really used to make you anxious, angry, or was a sure bet to get you to fly off the handle. Since Jesus moved into your life and spirit do you still react the same way? How surprising is that? As the days of the journey add up you find that you do not over-react to the things that used to set you off or ruin your day. Even under great stress you still possess underlying peace.

Until new habits of focus and understanding are solidly in place there will still be times when you have to decide which option is the right one and which is the wrong one. If you're a parent it's a good bet you were far more nervous and fretful over your first baby than your third. As new experiences become routine your response transitions from a hand-wringing dilemma to one of unconscious habit.

~

God does not call His children to obedience. God calls us to love His Son.

> *"He who has My commandments and keeps them, it is he who loves Me." – John 14:21*

Following the rules isn't the beginning of love. Think of anyone you truly love. Now, think of the last time you went out of your way to injure them. Did you say something particularly nasty to your husband (wife)? Did you gleefully break your child's favorite toy to savor his tears?

Love is the beginning of good not evil. It isn't possible for any person to perfectly act in love all the time. People aren't that honest with themselves, that sensitive, that perceptive, or that selfless. But New Creations in Christ are more so than anyone who does not love Jesus. Christians are to be known first *by their love* for one another (John 13:35).

Obedience is freely given

It is not possible to be obedient unless there is an option to NOT obey. Being forced to act is coercion, relying on intimidation or brute strength to obtain compliance. God never makes you do anything. Sometimes you might wish He would, but He does not.

The third item on the list of what God wants from you is the gift of obedience because you love and trust Him. Isn't that the same thing you want from your horse? Your children?

Obedience is a flower that blooms in a garden free of the weeds of fear. The methods for building faith in either horse or Christian are essentially the same. Fear cannot enter where faith abounds.

New Creations are on a journey to eliminate fear as faith in Jesus Christ increases. CHT is the journey of relationship between a worthy leader and a special horse that builds faith strong enough to transform a flighty prey animal into a bold confident horse that will stand its ground because its leader said that all was well.

Why choose obedience?

Factors that affect one's willingness to obey can also produce the opposite reaction. In some instances they result in a "yes" while in others "no." Doesn't it seem odd how one thing can motivate or de-motivate?

Here are a few examples of such factors:

- Effort
- Correction
- Cost
- Discomfort
- Loss

Effort is usually a de-motivator. Effort expends energy. Most horse owners decide not to ride or play with their horses at one time or another because the amount of effort required to change clothes, get to the barn, groom, and saddle seems greater than the immediate benefit. The older you get the heavier the saddle becomes. The eyes aren't the first to go, it's the strength to lift a stock saddle onto a horse that seems to somehow get taller every year.

More folks regret *not making* the effort and missing out on the opportunity to spend quality time with their horse than regret *making* the effort. At the end of your life the moments you most cherish will be moments shared with loved ones, 2- and 4-legged. The greatest regrets people have are the precious moments missed because the effort at the time seemed too much compared to the benefit.

Humans are very fickle creatures. As a full time trainer I never gave effort a thought. I got up, dressed, and messed with horses until I fell into bed well after dark. That was my routine, responsibility, and the cycle of my life. I rarely considered how much effort it took and whether or not it was worth it.

Well, there was one time. Breeding season was well underway. Foals were being born, mares bred, and the list on my refrigerator door detailed twenty-seven daily vet treatments I had to do. There were a couple of horses in isolation that made everything more complicated, but no one was seriously ill so it was more an energy drain than anything else.

Then a letter arrived from everyone's favorite, the Internal Revenue Service, notifying us of a business tax audit. I called my accountant who said he would have it delayed until after breeding season. My reply was, "No! Send the agent out to the ranch. I'm tired – maybe he'll shut me down!"

The afternoon the agent visited I gave him a tour of the place and identified every horse; which stallions belonged to clients, which mares were in to foal or breed, the horses in for training, and the ones who belonged to our program. He got to see the feed bins, hay barn, breeding lab, arenas, round pens, and even met our miniature tease stallion, Sparky. I explained that Sparky and I took a walk twice a day to chat with all the visiting girls and see if their "moods" were changing.

After our extensive walk we headed into the house for

something to drink and to continue the audit. Once we were settled I pulled out a printed sheet of paper listing the thousands of times we fed horses and cleaned stalls each year, how many tons of pellets and hay we delivered to hungry faces, how many vaccinations and injections I gave, the numbers of times I wormed horses, and then I showed him my list of twenty seven vet treatments for each day. That was followed by a quick overview of my training schedule, judging trips, and the show circuit we followed.

After reviewing my less-than-extensive staff we settled back to rest for a moment. He asked, "What do you do in your spare time?"

Before I had a chance to answer he corrected himself. "What a stupid question. You don't have any spare time." That was the moment I told him bluntly that I purposefully wanted him to visit us because I was tired, and if he thought I was indulging a hobby and not a business, I encouraged him to shut me down on the spot.

He didn't. In fact, after the audit we got a nice check from the government.

That was the only time I remember that the effort of the work nearly overwhelmed us. There were more times when frustration and loss made us wonder if it was all worth the massive cost in emotional energy of failure, death, and disappointment. But hindsight being what it is, I know that it took repetitive, profound, and sometimes painful obstacles to finally bring me to my knees and quit trying to do it all on my own. I gave it over to Jesus Christ.

My journey with Christ began long, long before that moment. But there was an actual event that made me realize I had no power to do what was required of me on my own. God's power alone could make me able, not the strengths, talents, or determination I brought to the table. It was the day fear departed. Like my dog Blue, I became fixated on the Giver and the gifts lost their lure.

My early life was a series of highs and lows – weighted on the side of more lows from my point of view. But through each one God taught me that there was always a way out; a way back; a solution that released me from the problem. All I had to do was persevere. Keep trying. Look to Him.

The Necessity for Reflexive Obedience

Why is reflexive obedience so important? Why is faith that generates obedience without thought the goal of the Holy Spirit for each Christian's journey of sanctification? What makes it a treasure worth searching for?

When a crisis comes, any doubt or delay may be fatal. Reflexive obedience does not require a horse or human to focus on the problem at hand and consider which response is best. Race car drivers react to imminent danger without thinking. Habit moves the steering wheel or applies brakes. Experienced horse trainers react to the movements of a horse automatically to balance, support, or stop.

When danger jumps in front of your horse on the trail, you want him to respond to your direction or thought without having to consider, debate, or focus. If his response to you isn't automatic it may be too late.

A barn fire is the best analogy I can think of to illustrate the importance of transformative relationship which builds faith to banish fear by reflexive obedience. Most horses perish in flaming barns because they refuse to leave the security of their stalls to enter what they considered a larger danger - the fire beyond. The horse that will not leave the barn has a greater fear of the fire than faith in the one who tries to lead him to safety.

Will your horse follow you through fire? What would happen if your horse was trapped in a burning barn? Does your horse have enough faith in you to overcome his fear if a fire threatens his or her life?

Are you afraid of the times we live in? Do you have enough faith in anyone to lead you to safety? Jesus Christ will come to lead you home at just the right moment. Do you trust Him enough to put fear behind and follow? Obedience is a product of relationship, not the rational evaluation of a request that has been considered and deemed reasonable. When the call comes, 'Yes' will save.

The promises of a worthy master are certain.

> *"Be strong and of good courage; do not be afraid, nor be dismayed, for the* LORD *your God is with you wherever you go." – Joshua 1:9*

> *For He Himself has said, "I will never leave you nor forsake you." – Hebrews 13:5*

The longer you walk with Jesus and the greater your love for Him grows the more automatic the journey becomes. Conscious decisions become fewer as you and He walk in one set of footprints in the sand. Your faith and familiarity with His character, His rhythms in your day, and His ability and commitment to deliver on every promise made become routine, automatic, and obedience to His will becomes reflexive.

There is nothing more fundamental in the Christian life than devotion to the Person, Jesus Christ, and recognizing how total His commitment is to you. He loved you first.

The same experience of reflexive response in transformative relationship with Christ is mirrored in the one you seek with your horse. It is not the same – nothing in this world equates to your walk with Christ – but there is nothing that is apart from it either. Early in your relationship your horse will not respond perfectly or immediately to a rein or leg cue. Transitions from one gait or direction to another will be conscious and deliberate. The longer you enjoy the journey of right relationship with your horse the more automatic many actions will become.

Have you ever marveled at the intensity of relationship between some children and their ponies? How can an untrained and unskilled little kid create a deeper and more profound relationship with a horse than most top trainers? Horses recognize that the love offered by the child is real and his or her spirit pure. Faith between child and pony grows on a foundation that does not recognize another alternative. Horses have no hidden agenda and neither do children.

"But Jesus said, "Let the little children come to Me, and do not forbid them; for of such is the kingdom of heaven." – Matthew 19:14

Perfect faith is easy for a little child. Worldly intelligence and error has not muddied their relationship processes yet. Jesus told his disciples that unless we rid ourselves of worldly wisdom and self-consideration we cannot enter the kingdom of heaven. Self interest and the pollution of the world make it very difficult to offer and keep even a simple promise to a horse. Transformative relationships are so committed that no other option exists. Horses recognize the difference – and so does the Holy Spirit.

The further along the path of transformative relationship you travel with Jesus Christ the narrower it becomes. The steps that lead you along are so small and the transition so gradual you don't recognize or admit any restriction. Even if you did you wouldn't care; you are exactly where you want to be.

There will be bumps and corrections along the road. The ability to maintain perfect focus amid the temptations and distractions of the world grows a bit at a time. Faith increases every time you overcome a bump and are refined by correction. Every obstacle removed reveals how much more is still possible. At the end of the journey you will find an unobstructed view of heaven.

CHT – INTRO TO PRACTICAL APPLICATION

"Movement starts as an unseen energy. It is an impulse which starts in the mind." - Training Horses Naturally

The ultimate goal of transformative relationship is for two to walk as one, where just a thought or suggestion of a request is more than sufficient to get the desired response. Suggestions may also be thought of as pre-cues. When a suggestion does not get the desired response the request is made more directly. *Please do it now.*

If a 'yes' answer is not given you must decide whether your horse is unable or unwilling to do as you asked. If he can't do as you ask you must help him become able. If he can, but simply won't, then you must take immediate action. You will either ask for a smaller response to get back to the habit of success or you will insist on the correct response by taking the smallest action necessary to achieve it.

Make Able ~ Motivate ~ Move On

Knowing which is the proper choice is a matter of knowing your horse and having a precise plan for what you hope to achieve.

Invitations, Questions, Requests, and Commands

There is a huge difference between asking a question, extending an invitation, making a request and issuing a command. I may invite my horse to come over to visit. The invitation is casual and comes with no hidden agenda. There is no right or wrong answer. It is a simple invitation. If the horse comes I will tarry for a moment; if not I will move on.

- Invitations are optional.
- Questions seek information.
- Requests expect a "Yes," and
- Commands are not optional.

Sometimes you will ask a horse a question for no other purpose except to learn the answer. *If I pick up the right rein three inches how will you respond?* There is a difference between a question and a request even though the terms are often used interchangeably in discussions about horse training. For the topic at hand you need to distinguish between the two.

The question *"What will you do?"* is far different than a request to *Give to the pressure on the right rein.* The first seeks an answer whatever it happens to be while the second expects a "yes."

Making a request comes with an expectation of an affirmative visible response. When I ask my horse to "Come" I expect his feet to begin moving in my direction. If hooves don't move there is a reason; the horse is either unable or unwilling to come. No matter the reason it is my responsibility to fix the problem. I will either make him able, or motivate him to move his feet.

No action is like Mom telling Richard, "Stop that. I mean it. "Of course she doesn't really mean it. There is no power in her request to Richard to quit.

If Richard couldn't hear her then he was unable to comply. Mom has the option to let Richard keep doing whatever is annoying her or she needs to move her own feet and remove her son's headphones and ask again. If he still refuses she needs to move his feet – briskly.

You may only ask one question at a time. Do not make a request unless you are 95% sure your horse will respond correctly and have Plan B ready in a moment should he fail. The transition from Plan A to Plan B should be seamless.

Making a direct request to a horse isn't much different. Be sure your request was heard and understood. If it was and feet don't move, get up and move the horse's feet – briskly. If it is truly necessary to issue a command to your horse, action is required on your part to improve the foundations of relationship, not to become a tougher autocrat.

Our Master knows us better than we know ourselves. When you ask a horse to obey you should know what response he is most likely to give as well as a list of other possible responses. Implementing the correct Plan B proves to your horse that you understand him and are always one step ahead of him. Faith is built on a foundation of confidence in your leadership.

The habit of success is built on tiny steps of success that

predictably follow one another. If the slightest refusal is answered with brisk movement there is little chance that a major refusal will pop up later. Fix each tiny inability or unwillingness and the relationship will progress smoothly and consistently.

One very difficult skill to master is knowing whether to ask a question or make a request. Even when that hurdle is cleared there is the weighty matter of which question to ask or what to request. Assuming you have determined which question or request to ask or make, the next challenge is discerning whether or not the horse has given you the right answer or response.

Do not take this lightly. In every round pen program I've done, regardless of the experience or level of achievement of those in attendance, the most frequently asked question is, "*How do I know what question to ask?*" Experienced trainers and neophytes alike ask the same question.

Too much knowledge about something can make it difficult to be simple, making some challenges more problematic for those with the most experience than those with little. Too many years of assumptions can muddy what must be clear calm water in order to be most effective. Horses seek simplicity and so do Christians. *Come as little children.*

A common prayer sent to heaven asks God to *make the right choice clearly right and the wrong choice clearly wrong.* Isn't the same desire for simple clear direction exactly what horses expect from you - what they hope for?

Victory by Perseverance

Success with a first small challenge introduces the concept of victory. Achievement is based on climbing a series of tiny steps one after the other followed by a chain of greater steps. With each successive step attained, the habit and history of success grows and with it faith to master whatever comes next.

As is the case with Tire Mountain, this obstacle at Brave Horse Center requires many initial steps before asking a horse to climb to the summit.

Mendi Hartung and Twister

Obstacles that may appear the most difficult to an observer may simply be one additional small step to the one taking it. The path leading to any feat that amazes, like Tire Mountain or jumping large cross country courses, is long, incremental, and noteworthy for its consistent small achievements.

In some cases, when faith is greatest, an obstacle may truly be extraordinary. But God will not ask you to master it unless He first makes it possible. Faith will level the tallest mountain.

"For assuredly, I say to you, if you have faith as a mustard seed, you will say to this mountain, 'Move from here to there,' and it will move; and nothing will be impossible for you. – Matthew 17:20

By faith in a worthy leader, both horses and New Creations in Christ do what others deem impossible.

"But Jesus looked at them and said, "With men it is impossible, but not with God; for with God all things are possible." – Mark 10:7

Horses do not obey out of fear. If obedience is not a choice it is the product of coercion. Submitting to a request to escape pain or fear chooses the lesser of two evils. Just as light and darkness cannot coexist, evil cannot be present in transformative relationship.

Humans who submit to the rule, restriction, and doctrine of a religion based upon fear will not receive the gift of faith. Fear and faith do not share the same space. They are mutually exclusive.

Horses willingly offer obedience to a worthy leader because lessons and conversations are designed to build faith, not skills. Horses learn from the systematic application and release of pressure, whether positional, spiritual, or physical. Properly prepared lessons or conversations that include the application of pressure rarely elicit anger, anxiety, or aggression.

Obedience replaces pressure with confidence. Faith builds as the horse learns that every promise is true and every puzzle has a solution.

Why do we offer obedience to God? Because of the gift of faith that informs us that fear is silly. Remember, the only two reasons a Christian has to fear anything is (1) fear that God can't handle the problem, or (2) fear that God won't handle the problem the way you want Him to.

Faith knows that God CAN and God WILL handle every need. Whether He does it to our liking is immaterial. Hindsight always proves that His way was better than ours, even if that hindsight won't be seen on this side of eternity. My favorite Garth Brooks song is, "Thank God for Unanswered Prayers." Amen!

Offering obedience to God isn't a sacrifice; it is the natural overflow of what Oswald Chambers calls "super-abounding devotion." Devotion and commitment drive side-by-side on a two way street. Both Master and man are devoted and committed in transformative relationship as are human and horse. Every time we assert authority over anything or anyone else we must yield equally in humility before Christ.

Jesus was so devoted and committed to you that He died on the cross that you might have eternal life. Is it so hard to believe that the devotion and commitment we have for Him would naturally produce obedience?

Worthy leaders are as devoted and committed to their followers (whether 2- or 4-legged) as is humanly possible. There are no deal-breakers and no desire to be excused from the investments of time, treasure, and emotional and physical energy required to keep every promise made.

TEACHING YOUR HORSE TO YIELD

In an earlier section we discussed reflexive obedience. Automatic obedience is the product of a relationship built on faith in a worthy leader. The process that builds faith is one of pressure and release; building a habit and history of meeting obstacles and overcoming them.

What does this process look like when you train a horse? I'll describe a series of steps. This list isn't exhaustive because an infinite number of steps could be added between each of these, but I hope it illustrates how the cycle of pressure – release builds the horse's faith in itself and in its master/leader.

Yielding Head and Neck

First Exercise - Step 1

Once a horse is confident in showing up, focusing, and secure with my attention and touch I often stand on the near side of the horse at his shoulder and pet his neck. Then his head. Then I briefly set the whole palm of my left hand on the top of his face where the nose piece of a halter usually sits.

Every move is made rhythmically and deliberately. There is

no pressure greater than a soft pet. I never take a new step unless the horse is peaceful and happy with the last. I repeat every step until the horse recognizes that we have advanced in our journey of communication and that I continue to live up to every promise made.

Step 2

After resting my hand on the bridge of the horse's nose I apply just enough pressure to suggest he move his head toward me. I remove my hand the instant he makes the slightest response, pet his neck once, and repeat the exercise. My hand rests atop the bridge of his nose until he responds just a bit. This is where patience isn't just a virtue but a necessity.

Within moments most horses begin to bring their head and neck my direction before my hand even touches their face. They figure my hand is coming up to ask them to yield and they offer obedience before I finish asking the question.

Using a series of steps I eventually ask the horse to bring his head and neck around to where I stand at his shoulder using a tiny cue with just my hand. Somewhere during the process I switch sides back and forth so both of the horse's eyes learn at the same pace.

Step 3

After the horse is responding easily to my hand I use a simple length of cotton rope. I have an assistant trainer named Ol' Red, the red remnant of a lead rope that lost its snap years ago. Red comes in handy for all the early training stages and as an insurance policy when working horses without any other tack or tools and both on the ground or mounted.

Ol' Red is draped over the horse's muzzle like a loose halter noseband and the process repeats step by step. The first step is for the horse to show no negative reaction to the rope. It goes over the nose and off... over the nose and off... over the nose and off. When the horse is ready I put the loose rope over the nose and move my hand toward my body only until the far side of the red loop touches the offside of the horse's muzzle like a side pull. The instant the horse gives his head one bit in my direction the red rope falls off his nose. And so on...

Step 4

The next step might be to put Red around the horse's neck midway between ears and withers. The process repeats until the horse softly learns to curve around to face me with his eyes.

Step 5

Once the horse freely yields his head and neck toward me I will continue asking until he has moved one foot in my direction simply from the touch of the rope the other side of his neck and my *suggestion*. The instant one hoof moves toward me I stop asking. He said 'yes' – what more could I ask? This action is repeated until the horse steps easily in my direction with his front end. Again, train both sides equally.

At this point the horse and I have a history of quiet success. The horse has never once experienced anger, anxiety, or aggression and I haven't worked too hard either. Yet the horse has already learned that the slightest pressure needs only a slight response to find the place of no pressure at all. Every step adds to our vocabulary as well as a foundation of movements to build upon later.

Pressure and touch are not the same. Applying pressure to a horse doesn't mean we have to make contact with him. The goal of CHT is progressive, when touch alone, without pressure, is sufficient to communicate a request to our horse. His obedience to touch is the step right before obedience to a gesture with no touch. And from there we advance to obedience by just a suggestion or thought – or purposeful look.

Yielding Hindquarters

The second fundamental exercise I teach horses is to yield the hindquarters away from me. The easiest physical reaction for a horse to make when his head and neck are slightly curved in my direction, as I stand parallel to his hindquarters and add a tiny bit of energy, is to step away which is exactly what I ask for.

Exercise Two: Step 1

Pressure on the hindquarters begins with the tiniest pressure possible, a precise purposeful look directly at the hips. Eventually I want intention alone to be enough pressure to elicit the desired response from my equine partner. If that's my goal then that is where I have to start.

Positional Power

If a direct stare at the horse's hindquarters isn't enough then I increase positional pressure. That means I make ME bigger. I suppose you could also say it is an increased pressure in energy. By energizing the space between me and the horse's hindquarters I am applying *positional* power. Once your horse understands this non-tactile and non-verbal method of communication it becomes a foundational tool.

Once a horse understands the questions I ask, all it takes to get the response I desire is to *look purposefully*. Just the energy created by my eyes settling specifically on a body part coupled with a gesture or *click-click* should get that body part to move.

Positional power is a function of gestures, energy, and intruding into someone else's space. Horses use this type of body language every day. Great horse communicators learn to use the vocabulary horses understand from birth to translate *words of movement* into new *words of position*. We learn to connect the body language of horses with requests for specific movements.

Step 2

If simply applying positional power doesn't work (and early on it won't) I add a slight tap on the hips. That usually does the trick. Think about Helen Keller and Annie Sullivan. Annie taught blind and deaf Helen to recognize that finger-spelling was a new way to communicate something tangible. The first connection Annie made with

Helen was "spelling" the word water in Helen's hand while holding it under running water.

Connecting Pressure and Conceptual Learning

Annie used a physical means to teach a concept. The use of pressure and release to teach horses is really quite similar. Helen's first reaction when she felt Annie's finger move deliberately in her palm was to try and snatch her hand away from the odd pressure, but Annie held it there until she made a connection. Helen learned that finger movements meant something precise. Horses learn that expressions and touch also mean something precise.

With his head and neck already curved in my direction the application of hip pressure naturally motivates the horse to step away from it. That means he steps his hind end away. That is exactly what I want so I QUIT asking. The instant one hoof moves away I accept the win and stop asking.

This process is repeated on both sides until just my look causes the horse to shift his hindquarters away. There is no pressure on his head, just little Ol' Red draped over his neck, and all I have to do is look at his hips and over they go. With consistent practice the horse will begin to respond correctly anywhere and anytime, without so much as a touch.

Step 3

Just as I did when teaching the horse to yield his head, neck, and forequarter to me with little more than intention, I do the same with his hind quarters. Once he knows that moving one hoof is the right answer I will continue to ask the question until he moves two; then three. And on we go. Every step of every exercise builds vocabulary and the habit of success through obedience.

Always teach both sides of the horse at the same pace. Pressure and release. Rhythmic and soft. Every step mastered adds to a history and habit of success. The horse learns from the beginning of our first conversation to respond to suggestions, not to demands or threats.

Teaching the Horse the Basic Command to Yield – Backing Up

Exercise Three Step 1 –

If your horse will move his forequarters and hindquarters whenever you ask you are halfway home. The next exercise is teaching the horse to back away when you stand just off of dead-center front.

Facing my horse just off center to the right (near side) I begin the exercise by petting his face and letting him know we're starting a new lesson. The position I prefer is about two feet in front of his head. The first actual cue I use is to purposefully look at his front feet and use my verbal cue for "move."

The cue I use for "move" is a cluck or click of the tongue usually associated with asking for a trot. It's a two beat cue – *click click* - and is a generic sound that my horses learn means "move whatever I'm looking at." When asking for a hip to move I use the *click-click* noise. When asking for the horse to back away I use the same cue. What differs is my intention – the focus and direction of energy. In this case I look at his feet and ask him to *click-click* move.

Early in a relationship with a horse he may not know exactly what *click-click* means and how to interpret my *purposeful* look. I usually allow a count of three for a horse to respond. If he doesn't I ask again with a little more energy. In addition to my purposeful look and *click-click* I might add a set of marching gestures with my hands directly in front of my body. Bigger body language sends movement and energy into the space between me and the horse. The series of cues repeats until ONE HOOF moves backwards. That is the right answer so I quit asking and tell the horse he did a good job.

Step 2 –

Once the horse understands what I mean the request gets a little bigger; I ask for a full backward stride. Once all four feet have moved I QUIT asking because the question was asked and answered perfectly.

Step 3

From there we build a longer back up; a more energized back up; and cues **get smaller rather than larger.**

Once my horses understand the vocabulary of movement it gets easier to expand the variety of movements I can ask for. As our history and habit of success continues to grow my horses move with very little body language or direct cues.

The finished conversation about backing up looks something like this: I stand somewhere toward the front end of the horse looking at his front feet and *click-click* with my tongue. Hooves should move. The more intent the look the more energy the horse should use to move backwards. When his response isn't what I intended I use slightly bigger cues until feet move.

Asti backing up. Photo – Kalena Randall

Asti knows I am *purposefully* looking at her front feet to square her up to be mounted. The intensity of my stare should be enough to move them, and as you see, it is. If her feet didn't move I would *click-click* to add more energy.

Discernment:

Discernment is the key to successfully building faith. If I ask one of my horses to back up using a tiny little cue and he does not I have to figure out why – in a very short period of time. If he is being lazy and pretty much just doesn't want to move I give him a second cue that is a tiny bit bigger. If feet don't move then I may skip all the way from a little cue to a BIG cue that may include actually touching him. I escalated because he was unwilling and it was my job to motivate him and be crystal clear about my intent.

What you do with your horse ALWAYS depends on what he did or didn't do after you asked a question or made a request. Teaching is a conversation. Relationship is a conversation filled with the ups of being totally connected on a spiritual level to the strange down of looking at one another as if someone suddenly started speaking in tongues.

Faith Increases Progressively

Faith in my leadership builds because the horse's own experience proves I only ask for small incremental responses and reward each try with peace and affection. The habit and history of our journey so far is one of success, confidence, quiet, and communication. I appreciate what the horse offers and he begins to respect and rely on my ability to move his feet and teach him new words and skills without any angst. It is a dance of joy.

Some horses are severely injured when they get caught in barbed wire fencing and panic. Others systematically and quietly try to figure a way out or calmly wait for help. The first horse reacts from fear, the second from faith. Thankfully I have not experienced the former with one of my own horses, but I have had the pleasure of several horses who were equine counterparts of Dennis the Menace. Whether caught in a fence, pasture feeder, under a rail, in a torn blanket, or other predicament, all waited to be freed rather than struggle.

The most talented was Cowboy, a quarter horse gelding who caught a fence wire between hoof and shoe, got a bucket stuck over his neck until the handle was across his wither and the bucket itself looked like a one-sided bra, somehow got an overturned pasture feeder with hay rack stuck over his back, and actually caught his jaw in a stirrup while standing on a hot walker. That one took the cake. I eventually saw him from the arena and rode over to see why he was curled up like a pretzel.

The stirrup was lodged in his lower jaw kinking his neck around to the side. The panic snap at the end of the walker rope was in his mouth behind the stirrup so I could not unsnap it. Cowboy stood there patiently. I admit I was impressed by his nonchalance.

In order to get to the walker rope snap I had to take the saddle apart. While I unbuckled the fender and pulled the whole thing off the saddle Cowboy's head was still stuck at his side. His neck was sweating on that side, but otherwise he was completely calm. After the stirrup and fender were free I was able to get his jaw out and then get into the back of his mouth to unsnap the rope.

I told Cowboy he was silly, bent his neck around to the other side a few times to stretch it out, reattached the fender and stirrup to the saddle and rode him.

Cowboy's experience from his first lesson until the walker incident was consistent. There was always a way out of every bind and there was always a place of perfect release. All he had to do was persevere and wait. When a horse learns to give to or be supported by pressure, he learns that there is always a solution to a problem and as long as he perseveres in his attempts to find the answer he will.

Faith that is hidden isn't faith. Faith that eclipses fear is worn on the sleeve. Faith that is greater than political correctness or expediency is on display for the entire world to see. Faith that saves is exhibited in what is said as well as in what is done or NOT done.

COMMUNICATION - THE TRAINING CYCLE

The level of your horse's concentration will always be one notch below your own. The degree of precision your horse gives to you depends entirely on how precise you are. Before you initiate any training session you must be very clear about what you want to accomplish and how you intend to achieve your goal.

- What question or request are you making – precisely?

- Describe the response your horse will make if he says 'yes' to your request.

- If your horse says 'no' what is your back-up plan?

- What question or request will you make the instant your horse says 'no'?

- Describe the response your horse will make if he says 'yes' to your new request.

- If your horse says 'no' what is your back-up plan?

The cycle of ask and answer continues until you get a willing 'yes' from your horse or you realize you really don't have a plan.

Even partners in committed relationships feel deep frustration when there is a failure to communicate. CHT requires you to be precise.

- How do you want your horse to respond? Exactly how.

- Where do you want his feet to go? Exactly where.

- Which foot do you want him to move? Exactly how much or in which direction?

- How quickly do you want him to move? Precisely how quickly.

Some of you might think that's a lot of detail to put into a plan. We're just getting started. Since your horse can't concentrate or be any more exact than you are there are a few more details that must be nailed down. Here are a few case studies.

Have a Plan

God had a fully developed plan before He spoke the heavens and earth into existence. His plan was perfect until Adam and Eve decided they had a better idea. God already had a back-up in place - His name is Jesus.

What are you going to do with your horse today once you're tacked up and ready to mount? Do you have a plan?

Every time you are in the company of your horse you either teach him something new, reinforce a lesson learned, or a little of both. Continued success and consistency depends on practice, practice, practice. That means you have to have a plan.

Your plan may be as simple as *ride to the pond and back at a walk*. You don't care how your horse gets you there or gets you back as long as you make it to the pond and back to the barn. Most riders fail to recognize that a plan that loose and imprecise means they **may not** correct the horse for any reason other than breaking gait, failing to get to the pond, or ending up somewhere other than where you began.

Do not expect your horse to perform at any level higher than you asked him to. This seems pretty simple but it is not. When you horse is obedient it is a huge temptation to forget about your simple goal and decide to ask your horse for just a bit more. The first step on the road to failure is to change the rules midway through the game.

Remember **Unbreakable Rule #1**: When your horse does what you ask QUIT asking.

Here is a step-by-step outline for setting the goal of riding a circle to the left. Most folks see this as a very simple goal that won't frighten too many horses, but "ride a left circle" IS NOT enough for a plan.

Step-By-Step – Ride a left circle.

1. Where does the circle begin?

2. Where will it end?

3. How many times are you going to ride the circle?

4. How big of a circle will you ride?

5. What gait will you ride? A laid back or forward walk, trot, or canter?

6. Does it matter if your horse simply makes it around or will you require something a bit more precise? How precise?

7. If your horse fails to be as precise as you want, what is your plan to correct him?

8. How are you going to get to the spot where you will begin your circle? Gait? Path?

9. What are you going to do when you are finished riding the left circle? Are you going to stop? Transition to a different gait? Continue working?

Unless you plan to park your horse at the end of the circle and leave him there you need to consider what you plan to do when this part of the lesson is finished. If you plan to continue working after completing the left circle begin a new list of questions to precisely plan the next stage of your lesson. Factoring in regular *stop and smell the roses* breaks makes planning simpler.

When I plan to ride a circle I imagine an actual white line or tracing on the ground so I know if my horse's feet are landing precisely on the circle, and if not, how far off the circle we wandered so I can ask for a more precise response the next time.

TIRE MOUNTAIN

Tire Mountain is the ultimate obstacle at our place. The mountain was created with a bunch of different sized tires placed together and packed with sand. It consists of a series of gradual steps of tires from smaller and shorter to bigger and taller. Few horses would be willing to climb the tire steps to the summit if not properly prepared.

Would any of my horses climb to the top the first time I asked without proper preparation? I'll never know because I will never ask.

Reaching the top of Tire Mountain is a journey. The fun of the attempt is in the series of successes enjoyed with my horses along the way. If the day comes when they all pop up to the top without thinking, I'll make the mountain bigger. The joy is in the journey, not getting to the top.

Goals may have dozens or hundreds of preparatory steps. Creating the history and habit of success demands that steps are small enough to guarantee success without anger, aggression, or anxiety. I will illustrate such progression with the steps I use on the way to Tire Mountain.

Tire 101 – the horse gets to play at liberty with one tire on the ground.

Tire 102 - the horse is asked to walk over, through, or around one shallow tire. All he has to do is get from one side to the other.

Gauntlet 101 – the horse is asked to walk between two long parallel ground poles set about three or four feet apart. Once he walks through one way he is asked to walk through the opposite way. There is no speed requirement and there must always be slack in a lead rope if one is used. When the horse goes in one end and comes out the other he is 100% successful.

Gauntlet 102 – the horse walks through the poles again with one shallow tire between the poles. Again, as long as the horse goes into the space between the poles on one end and comes out the other he is successful. The lead must be slack and it makes no difference if the horse steps over, around, or in the tire.

Gauntlet 103 – I add a few more tires to the dirt between the poles. Again, as long as the horse goes in one end and out the other he is successful.

Gauntlet 104 – if your horse tends to hurry through the gauntlet ask him to stop somewhere along the way. After each step change the way the tires are arranged between the poles. Each step is so small most horses tend to get a little bored. By the time you get to this step you already have a series of five successes.

Gauntlet 105 – Set another pole across the top of the two parallel ground poles so the horse has to negotiate the tires and step over the pole.

Tire Bridge – from the Gauntlet the horse advances to parallel utility poles that border a series of tires of different height and width packed with dirt. The horse learns to go through, over, and negotiate terrain where each hoof is on a different plane. Again, there must be slack in the lead rope and as long as the horse enters the "bridge" on one end and exits on the other he is successful.

Single Tire – Once a horse is bored with the Gauntlet and Bridge we move on to the Single Tire, a large tractor tire about ten inches tall and four feet wide packed with dirt.

Single Tire 101 - the horse learns to step his front feet onto the tire platform and rest. I usually ask horses to dismount across the tire rather than backing up. I don't care if a horse feels the need to back off for a while, but eventually success involves a forward exit.

Single Tire 102 - the horse learns to walk up to the tire, up onto the tire, and over the tire in a straight line. Again, there must be no tension on the lead and no speed requirement.

Single Tire 103 – at this stage I ask the horse to rest with all four feet on the tire. It is a big step learning to balance three feet on one level while moving the first hoof off when asked to dismount.

Tire Hill – After Single Tire is mastered it's on to Tire Hill. Three sand-packed tires form steps from smaller to taller. Horses learn to climb up a short hill, turn, and step off confidently.

All the steps of Single Tire are repeated on Tire Hill. Only after the horse is pretty much bored by the process will we approach Tire Mountain. You should have a good idea of just how many steps are required before the horse is ever asked to climb to the top.

Reaching each tier of Tire Mountain includes every step in Single Tire until the horse finally rests on the summit.

Horses have to learn to balance climbing up and climbing down even shallow steps. Most terrain changes are far more gradual than Tire Mountain. Some horses can accomplish every step from Tire 101 to the top of the Mountain in one session. Each horse is allowed to progress at whatever speed he needs to be successful and confident at each step before moving on to the next.

When the journey to Tire Mountain is spread over a number of sessions I begin each new session several steps or obstacles earlier than the last one mastered in the previous lesson. Only move forward if your horse is calm and bold.

When you begin working tires from the saddle begin at the beginning and repeat each step. If you move on to Tire Mountain under saddle repeat each and every step. Just because your horse was able to balance his own body from the Gauntlet to Tire Mountain he may not be able to do so with you on board. Give him the chance to build up to the summit slowly.

Remember, the journey is your reward, not getting to the top of the Mountain.

CONSTRUCTIVE CORRECTION

Christian Horse Training (CHT) teaches the importance of discernment. As a worthy leader you must know where the correction ends and the crutch building begins.

Shiner is one of two Appaloosas God sent us to bring home in 2009 when they needed rescue. We sold Shiner and his brother Ace as babies to the same family. Nine years later they came home together. Shiner tells readers his side of the story - and I tell mine - in *He Came Looking for Me*.

A new journey of relationship began the day Shiner came home. Neither he nor his brother will ever be sold again. Shiner and Ace are home to stay. And thus we established a beginning.

Shiner did not return home with any usable skills. Shiner actually returned to our family with a spirit of hopelessness rather than anticipation. Shiner was so afraid of being separated from his brother that he couldn't go 30 feet away without having a panic attack. Shiner's dependency on Ace wasn't a vice or evidence of bad behavior. Shiner didn't need to break a bad habit; Shiner needed to learn hope.

The years since Shiner and Ace returned home have been fruitful. Shiner has found hope and his personality and spirit have found balance. That balance is the result of daily maintenance. It is possible for the foundations of personality to be permanently damaged by experience. Like the foundation of a building it must either be corrected or the limits of what is built on top of it will be severely restricted.

Shiner and I have slowly moved forward. When I started riding him our greatest challenge was simply moving forward - away from the barn and Ace. Shiner was willing to be saddled, mounted, and give to gentle pressure on a snaffle rein. He moved with me on his back without any huge concern – until I suggested he go forward and not just turn back, again and again, toward the barn.

Before long I could ride Shiner to the far end of the arena if we didn't stay there long. I remember how proud I was of him the first time I rode him all the way around the arena. The next hurdle was stopping and standing quietly in the furthest corner of the pen from the barn.

Building a foundation of relationship with Shiner followed the same process of transformative relationship as any other horse. All horses and riders will not make such a great commitment, and every horse doesn't require total commitment from the trainer to become a useful mount and member of the barn.

Commitments make promises. CHT is the process of making promises you are both able and willing to keep. Every time. Without exception. Always.

It isn't possible to be the perfect master to a horse. It is, however, absolutely imperative to try.

What do you call someone who breaks a promise? A liar. None of us will perform perfectly, but let the price of our error be on our own head and not the one to whom the promise was made. This is a requirement of properly balanced authority and humility.

"Why," some might say, "should I pay the cost of failure when the promise was made to a lowly horse?"

"Why," I might respond, "should Christ have paid the cost of your failure when He was sinless and you are guilty?" The horse is as blameless as Jesus. Neither should pay the price of our sin, yet our debt was paid. The least we can do – and must do – is to make commitments and promises wisely.

Horses that come to you unbalanced due to nature or experience can find security through transformative relationship. Unstable compounds require more careful handling than stable ones. Nitroglycerine is highly unstable and should only be managed by someone qualified to do so. Unstable personalities must be handled only by those who are both qualified to do so and willing to make the requisite commitment.

Shiner's future depends on my ability to keep the promise I made that nothing will ever hurt him and I will never ask him to something he cannot do. God knows each of us better than ourselves. He is the perfect Master. My goal is to know Shiner better than he knows himself and to anticipate how any lesson or experience will affect him.

Anxiety is Shiner's biggest problem. He wants a crutch to make his world right. Ace was that crutch for years. My plan was to transfer his dependence from Ace to me and then use that beginning to build his confidence in himself. My eventual goal is to eliminate Shiner's need for a crutch and to help him change, to become something different and something more than he was before.

Anxiety is a huge distraction that prevents Shiner from concentrating on what we're doing. Some horses are unwilling to pay attention; Shiner is frequently unable to stay focused when he becomes too emotional.

Aggression is the result of negative emotion in action. When horses become frightened their first instinct is to run. When a rider prevents the horse from doing what its emotions dictate, the flight response may change to a fight response. Aggression is often the picture of a fearful horse unable to flee what it perceives as danger.

Shiner is fully capable of resisting my plan. The first time I rode him through the open arena gate to the pasture he freaked. Our ride had gone very well and I thought he could handle one more small step. I was wrong. We returned to the arena and repeated the previous step until Shiner was no longer emotional.

Make the right thing easy

Many trainers and clinicians teach students to make the right thing easy and the wrong thing difficult for their horses. That is true, but you must correctly discern if the wrong response was given because the horse was unable to give the right one or because it was unwilling to give the desired response.

Knowing how to constructively respond to your horses is not as simple as "Do what I ask or I'll work you into a frothy sweaty mess." Horses can be drilled to make a point for two basic reasons;

1. To focus energy use on physical rather than emotional expression, or

2. To get the horse to focus more on your request than his own opinion of what he should be doing.

There's a big difference in the two. If a horse is already emotional don't pick a fight. If a horse is using its energy to resist you, give it something more useful to do with that energy. Using discipline or punishment to "correct" a fearful horse is always wrong.

Loping Shiner is a long term project still under construction. It was nearly a year before he could lope around a round pen at liberty without becoming too anxious. As his level of anxiety increased his ability to make it around without banging himself up decreased. We worked our way up, adding one stride at a time, until he had the confidence and ability to canter around the round pen just once without completely losing focus.

It took another year before Shiner could canter on a longe line. All during this time I had loped him under saddle on both leads, but only to keep the concept of loping within his universe of possibility. We didn't lope much, but we loped. Shiner's tendency to quit complicates the process of maintaining a lope. Because of my own physical limitations at the time, the program had to slow down enough to keep both of us safe and balanced.

One morning I rode Shiner in the arena and we were getting along pretty well. Because my arena has only three sides I like to circle on the far end to take advantage of the natural barrier when asking a horse to learn to balance and recognize framing cues at a brisk trot or canter with the least possible use of the reins.

When Shiner and I get serious about learning we head to the far end of the arena. This particular day all was progressing as planned until I kept Shiner at the far end of the pen a bit too long. As the number of circles increased so did his anxiety. Before long Shiner's focus on the work at hand decreased as his level of concern increased. Shiner was losing his emotional balance.

In order to make the right thing easy you have to first know what the right thing is. There's a difference between working to gain focus and working on circles. You can't work on circles if the horse is emotionally absent. I needed focus to work on circles so I used circles to regain focus. Shiner was unable to respond where we were so I moved us to a place where he could. We started working again just outside of the barn.

Many times I've let a horse that wanted to run to the barn or in-gate do so. The moment we arrived at the horse's destination of choice we worked harder. No punishment or correction, we just burned more energy. Once the horse was performing the maneuver correctly I gave it the opportunity to walk back to where it first made the decision to ditch to the gate or barn. Repeat that scenario often enough and most horses begin to realize that rejecting my choice of exercises was far more difficult than going with the flow.

Shiner's problem with maintaining focus is not because he is unwilling but because he is unable. Shiner wanted to go back to the barn. I didn't allow him to choose the direction and speed of escape, but we did go back to an area right outside the breezeway. Shiner's brain was somewhere inside the building and I needed to bring it back to me.

Showing a horse a pattern is a good way to calm it and return its brain back to a useful mode. I asked Shiner to walk a circle just outside the barn using just enough direction to make fairly consistent circles. I didn't care about the quality of the circles; I was trying to quickly establish a habit of task. If Shiner could easily do as I asked it would take less time to redirect his attention. As the number of quiet circles increased so did Shiner's ability to think. Before long he let out a huge breath and began thinking about what we were doing and not about being separated from the herd.

When Shiner's emotions blew up on him he was unable to focus on me. He did not deliberately refuse to work; he simply could not stay in the moment. Once his focus returned I used the now familiar circle pattern at a walk as the foundation for stepping up to a trot. We returned to the same exercise we'd been doing at the far end of the arena.

Once Shiner was working comfortably I trotted him back to

the far end of the arena. We circled there twice then trotted back to the barn with a nicely controlled cadence. After a circle at the barn we trotted back out into the arena again. Shiner stayed with me the rest of the ride and even stood at the end of the pen quietly. Our ride headed back to the barn before Shiner lost focus and got emotional again and trotted out to the end of the arena when he was confident and secure. Relationship and leadership is an art, not a science. The goal is always to keep emotions balanced and positive.

Emotions can be like avalanches; once they start careening downhill there's no way to stop them. The goal is to keep the avalanche from beginning. The trick with Shiner is to step in before he gets too far out of emotional balance – regroup – and continue building a habit of success instead of constantly fixing broken places.

The longer the periods of time between Shiner's moments of emotional drama the more confidence he builds in his own autonomy and ability to focus on me and not some place in his head. My goal is to help Shiner never get out of balance again, but it's a fine line and sometimes you have to press it to grow.

Correction is a useful tool for teaching how to do right things better. Once I earned a measure of Shiner's faith we started adding to his skill set. Shiner mastered the idea of moving forward. He is usually fine to ride out alone and hasn't had a panic attack in ages. As he learned to learn I was able to ask him to not only keep the color on the paper but to begin coloring within the lines.

Teaching Shiner to ride the rail

Once Shiner moved forward comfortably at a walk and trot it was time to teach him to keep moving without a constant cue of "stay between the reins." Shiner needs to find confidence in his own ability and increase the amount of time he is able to maintain his focus without a reminder from me. Shiner still has a slight tendency to quit moving when he feels that I am no longer actively concentrating on what he's doing. Horses can only concentrate and perform as precisely as the leader. It takes time and strong foundations for horses, especially those like Shiner, to learn to work independently.

At the beginning of this lesson series Shiner moved consistently and correctly on the arena rail or in any other direction or figure I asked for as long as I provided constant support with my legs and reins. Contact was always light, but if dropped for even a moment Shiner's internal gyro would kick in and we'd be heading a different direction before any two of his feet hit the ground again.

Shiner was better about working in a straight line when he was heading back towards the barn – no surprise – but the instant we turned up the rail away from the barn he couldn't travel six feet without supervision.

It was time to teach Shiner to be a bit more accountable for what he did and not to rely on the crutch of never-ending support. It was time to ask Shiner to step up and grow up. It was time to ask Shiner to ride on the rail without being held there.

One way I teach horses to work the rail independently is to establish a specific distance off the rail that will trigger a full and specific correction if the horse crosses it. Early in the lesson I use a distance of about ten feet; when the horse gets ten feet off the rail I pick up the outside rein and do as close to a 90 degree turn back to the fence as possible then another 90 degree turn to set the horse back in a straight line up the fence.

Asti on the rail without a crutch

If we're working the rail clockwise and the horse drifts far enough to the inside to touch the 10 foot line I pick up the left rein and do a purposeful ninety degree turn back to the rail. Just as the horse's nose meets the desired track along the rail I pick up my right rein and do another square turn to the right to set him back on the rail. The more precise and direct the correction the quicker the horse will understand what you're trying to communicate.

I started the exercise with Shiner at a trot. The moment I

sent him up the rail in a straight line I dropped my reins and gave him the opportunity to self-steer. It is important to look where you want the horse to go. I focused on a tree about a quarter mile away and let Shiner start to work on his own.

We didn't get three feet before he veered off the rail and we hit the 10 foot "line in the sand" in short order. I turned him back toward the fence then set him straight up the rail again and dropped the reins.

Same result. The instant I dropped the reins Shiner headed off the rail. Again, I turned him back to the fence and then back up the rail. We did it again and again. After you get the same result for a while you begin to question whether the lesson is working. As long as both you and the horse remain calm the right decision is usually to stick with it. If anyone's emotions start to rise it may be time to regroup.

The correction of making precise turns is a means of communication. Some horses take a while to figure out what you're asking and others almost make it a contest of who can out-stubborn the other. There is no place in this exercise – or any exercise – for punishment or heavy-hands. Keep at it precisely, always at the same 10 foot mark, and always drop the reins when the horse is on the rail track.

I admit I wondered if Shiner would ever get it. I've been in that place many times over the years. After a while he began to stay on the rail by himself when we were heading toward the barn. First he moved straight for 30 feet, then 50 feet, then 100 feet, then the whole side of the arena –

heading toward the barn.

When we made the turn and headed up the opposite rail it was the same old thing. Drop the reins and Shiner would ditch toward the middle. But even Shiner finally figured it out. On the rail going to the barn he was never corrected and got to keep moving loose and easy. He was beginning to build a new habit and didn't even know it.

I admit it took some more time, but eventually Shiner began to stay on the rail track longer or veered off less than 10 feet. Working at a trot offers a cadenced gait and there is less likelihood you'll mess up your horse's balance making those 90 degree turns. If your horse needs a break let him rest on the rail in the track you plan to travel when you're ready to work again.

I don't know if Shiner was confused or dumb like a fox. It didn't matter, but the light bulb finally went on. Shiner seemed to say, "Oh, is that all you wanted me to do?"

Correction is a means of setting boundaries. Success is incremental. First you learn to keep the color on the page, then inside the lines. Teaching a horse to ride the rail independently first asks the horse to stay within 10 feet of the rail, then 5, and eventually to stay in the rail track itself.

Shiner started to figure out that the right answer was to stay on the rail even when the reins were loose. Unless that lesson is repeated day after day the fragile connection made will be broken.

The three most important things in real estate are location, location, location. To create a new habit the three most important things are practice, practice, practice.

The program of incremental corrections that teaches Christians how to travel the path leading to the narrow gate of Matthew 7 is similar to the one used to teach kids to color or horses to ride the rail independently.

The entrance to the path New Creations travel on their walk with Christ is as wide as an ocean, infinitely broad and smooth. Simply going in the right direction is sufficient.

A beginning must be established before you start thinking about anything more precise. Boundaries are established and successes are incremental. Corrections occur along the way when the path ahead begins to narrow.

Just as Shiner had to learn to move forward on his own without quitting or running for the security of the familiar, Christians have to learn to step out onto and along the path without quitting and running for the familiarity and false-security of the world.

Correction builds Confidence

Never correct an effort in progress. Let your horse commit to a mistake before you correct his performance. Correction is not used to introduce or teach; it is used to make perfect.

The proper use of correction builds confidence in one's ability to both understand a goal and to perform successfully. Using correction as a crutch builds confidence in the crutch, undermining the strength available at the beginning. The continuous use of a crutch weakens rather than builds.

If you always ride your horse with a restricting rein you will always *have* to ride your horse with a restricting rein. Unless you give your horse the opportunity to fail it will never learn to succeed independent of the crutch of your hand. The only way your horse will ever learn to ride with a loose rein or no rein is to ride with loose reins or no reins.

2 yr-old Angelina on loose rein

Begin with a loose rein and worry about frame later. Angelina, by Invitation Only, is bred to be a western pleasure mare. Once she was secure at all three gaits on a loose rein I could begin to put her together. Her low head set in the photo above is the way she started. She's been performing in Europe with her new owner for several years.

The hands of a worthy master support and encourage; they do not serve as barriers to growth and confidence. The touch of grace empowers, it does not weaken.

Build a habit and history of success

"In any team sport, the best teams have consistency and chemistry." - *Roger Staubach*

The two bookends that support success are commitment and consistency. Precision and correction are essential tools to build consistent experience that produces success, one little bitty step after another. Every big success is the sum of a series of tiny successes. Consistency in the progressive mastery of skills is measured, planned, predicted, and is the result of a cast-in-stone commitment to building a habit and history of success. Confidence comes from achievement.

"With accomplishments come confidence and with confidence comes belief. It has to be in that order." – *Coach Mike Krzycwski*

If you follow a leader through one trial successfully you might be disposed to follow again. If you follow the same leader one hundred times and are successful every single time you will begin to have faith that every obstacle or lesson will be concluded successfully. Transformative relationship is the epitome of relationship chemistry.

The first time you lead your horse through a problem and he successfully finds the correct solution he is open to working with you a second time. By the time your horse has accumulated a history of one hundred successful lessons he will have both the habit and expectation of success in the next, and the one after that. Your horse will trust your leadership and have faith that in all things you will lead him to success.

Is your faith in Christ the result of a supernatural leap? No. Faith is a gift from God as well as the reasonable result of a history of experience that Christ is faithful in each and every trial. No obstacle is too great. The Bible is consistent. God is consistent. Relationship with Jesus Christ is a consistent blessing of progressive mastery of skills and blossoming faith.

FURTHER ALONG YOUR JOURNEY

Before you can register how much progress you are making in the journey of sanctification in Christ and as a worthy leader to your horse, there must be some form of measurement. Mile markers along the interstates of the United States make it easy to gauge how far you've come from where you began and how much of the journey remains before you reach your destination. Relationships are not as simple to evaluate as a road trip.

The ways people measure success differ depending on what is being measured. Money and material wealth is fairly easy to quantify. The difference between a savings account with a balance of $22 and one of $22,000 is specific and stated in terms most people understand. Whether one is rich or not based upon the balance in his savings account is another matter entirely. Being rich is a matter of definition or opinion, not measurement.

It isn't possible to accurately measure the progress of a journey unless you are 100% committed to it. How successful is a family if the husband is doing great, the wife pretty well, the son rather poorly, and the daughter is failing completely?

Well, it's not possible for the family to be doing well if one member is failing, you might say. You would be right. How can you begin to register the progress in your journey with Christ or with your horse if there are exceptions?

What happen in Vegas stays in Vegas

The ad campaign encouraging folks to behave completely outside of their normal parameters because they are in Las Vegas is popular because it is a salve to itching ears (2 Timothy 4:3). Some folks relish this message because they think it gives them permission to indulge their *natural lusts* when they think no one is watching and there will be no consequences.

The ad suggests that it is possible to eliminate accountability for behaving outside of the normal rules as long as you separate the time and location of your bad acts from your regular life. If what you do stays in Vegas no one who might hold you accountable will know, so it doesn't count. If it stays in Vegas the sin won't follow you home. It's a freebie!

That is a lie. There is no distinction between the secular and the sacred to New Creations in Christ. Any commitment made to spouse, family, or employer that is rendered void at the outskirts of Vegas isn't much of a commitment. You don't drop off the core values and directing spirit of your life in Henderson, Nevada and pick them up again on your way home. The truth is, your core values become evident by what you do in Vegas when no one is watching.

The corner stone of transformative relationship is commitment. Commitment is complete. There are no deal breakers, exceptions, or limits of jurisdiction. Commitment is everywhere, every day, and in every situation. Anything you bring to Vegas will be with you while in Vegas and will still be there when you walk through your front door at home again.

Compartmentalization

Compartmentalization is equally problematic when working with horses. When a horse puts up figurative yellow caution tape around part of its body or resists a particular situation there is an obligation to resolve the problem and tear down the tape.

Some horses say *You can't get on my left side*, or *Don't even think of using spurs on me buddy*, or *Pick up my hind feet at your own risk*, or *Touch that girth and I'll bite you.*

If you do not correct the situation when a horse sets a boundary past which you may not go it will become a crisis of faith. If you permit the horse to keep any place off-limits from you, his master, it proves that his fear is greater than your power. How much faith in God could you have if you could tell Him where He can and cannot go and His reply was, "Yes, ma'am" or "Yes, sir"?

Some trainers discover a problem area and immediately call out the big guns to attack and destroy it. Unless a horse bites, strikes, or kicks me I will not attack anything, ever. Horses do not warn or threaten from a place of strength but from a place of weakness. One does not attack a friend where he is most vulnerable. Predators exploit weak spots; a worthy leader/master will not.

God knows where we place our Off Limit signs. He notes them and then proceeds to build a greater foundation of relationship. That is the way I approach horses. I will not fail the horse by letting it keep its place of insecurity; I simply work on earning the horse's focus and trust.

Over the years I have discovered that most issues resolve themselves once a horse has learned to believe my promises. If a horse's body language tells me, *don't go there because I am afraid,* I am not going to fight the horse's fear by making it worse. I work to erase the fear by increasing the amount of faith the horse has in me.

The last place I focus my attention or actions with a horse that is cinchy is the girth. The last place I focus my attention on a horse that is head shy is his head. The last place I focus on a horse that refuses to pick up a foot is his feet. By the time I tighten a girth, mess around with ears, and pick up hooves the horse will have sufficient faith in me not to worry about girth, head, or feet.

Working with horses that block you

During one round pen program I worked with a horse with numerous issues. In fact, the horse's reputation was well known to all in the audience. I didn't have any problems with the horse… which proved that my message was true. During the program the gray mare made it clear that she did not want me on her off side. She was fine if I was on the near side but tried to block me moving to the opposite side.

Rather than try to sneak or push my way to the off side I simply went back to the center of the round pen and asked her to move in a clockwise direction. As long as she went around me to the right she earned a 100% score. She did. She walked. Sometimes she trotted. She rested. All the time her right eye was looking at me. The purpose of the exercise was to teach her right eye that it was perfectly normal for me to be on her off side and that nothing dangerous or emotional happened. It was a real ho-hum.

After a few minutes of being the focus of her right eye I stopped her. The last time I tried to move from stroking her neck on the near side of her body and then step across to the other side she blocked me. This time she didn't bat an eye. I didn't try to make her accept me in that eye; I simply allowed her right eye and brain to get used to the idea while at liberty.

What to do when what you're doing isn't working

Sometimes you simply get stuck. It happens. When forward movement looks more like backwards movement you have four options to choose from:

1. Keep doing what you're doing. Of course, you'll get the same results.

2. Take a break. Gain some perspective. Talk to someone who might help you figure out what's going on. One or both of you is unable or unwilling, but it can be difficult to diagnose your own situation once it's gotten a bit too sticky.

3. Change what you're doing. Make a plan to slow down and go back to a place, schedule, or routine that worked. Depending on the nature of your relationship with the horse

you will either go back and check each block in the foundation of skill training or revisit every block in the foundation of relationship until you find the one that is broken or went missing.

4. Quit. The End.

The two major factors that determine which of these options you select is (1) your level of ability to be an effective leader by keeping every promise made, and (2) your level of commitment to the relationship itself.

Sanctification: the path of increasing perfection

Total perfection does not exist in the world. No human performs perfectly in every challenge or enterprise of importance. Sooner or later our attention or feet will stray from the path directed by the Holy Spirit. Wandering thoughts and temptations of the flesh will draw us away from complete focus and obedience to God's will. Transformative relationship with God and horses is not a destination; it is a journey of joy.

Grace and mercy recognize these moments of distraction and correct them with love, patience, and supportive guidance. God knows your heart and your limitations. You are accountable to know the heart of your horse and his limitations. You are to grant grace and mercy in the same measure your Master grants it to you.

Years of relationship with horses gave me a context for processing my own walk with Jesus Christ. When challenged to identify where I am and whether or not I remain on the right path in God's eyes I flip the question from God and me to me and a horse. Usually that brings clarity and I can determine if the issue is one of inability or unwillingness. When it doesn't I know that patience is the best plan. Don't push. Wait.

Reining horses are defined as being *willingly guided*. One of the most grievous errors a reining horse makes is to anticipate a cue and jump into a maneuver the rider did not ask for.

Rope horses are scored in the box to produce patience and reduce anticipation. Reiners stand quietly in the center of the pen to teach the horse that one big move does not mean another will happen immediately afterwards. The right answer is always to be ready but not to act until the request is made.

Too many Christians focus on *doing* rather than listening. The journey of a New Creation in Christ is a wonderful illustration for properly training and providing great leadership to a horse. Early in the training process lessons are very simple and horses need frequent correction. Earlier in the book you read about the need to differentiate between correct responses and incorrect responses. Before you concentrate on subtle variations of the hue and saturation of color, you need to learn to recognize the lines on the page and keep the crayon marks inside them.

You can't take a proper first step unless you know which direction you're going. God does not expect us to read His mind and you fail your horse when you expect him to read yours. Communication is a give and take, back and forth exercise.

Am I doing what God wants me to? Are my feet still on the right path?

I ask myself these questions on a fairly regular basis. That's a good thing. Maintaining correct form, direction, and speed requires frequently looking around at the scenery. As your horse begins to carry himself properly and maintain his focus on you for longer periods of time your corrections will be fewer and more subtle. In the beginning I was thrilled when Shiner moved forward in a straight line for five feet before I had to correct him. He had the toughest time learning to color within the lines. Reins, seat, legs, balance, and vision establish the lines that tell your horse where to draw and which color to use.

As Shiner progressed he learned to move in a straight line for twenty feet, then fifty, and then one hundred. Each accomplishment was a success that strengthened a habit of success. The roadblocks to Shiner's ability to stay on the path I directed were distractions of emotion and established negative habits, as was the temptation to turn back to the barn and the rest of the herd. Shiner didn't overtly resist or refuse my requests; he just could not focus on them for a long period of time.

The promises I made Shiner meant I would never ask him to do something I did not first prepare him to do. It is my responsibility to make him able. Obedience is not possible if one is unable to offer it. God as Master knows us better than we know ourselves and never fails to make us able to do as He asks.

As Shiner and I move forward I don't have to correct him

as often. Reins and legs are more supportive in nature and offer gentle reminders of where the lines are on the page. As his skills improve and our methods of communication expand he will be able to respond to more conceptual requests rather than specific ones. Instead of picking up a red crayon and coloring in the outline of the bucket on the paper I will be able to say, *Shiner, draw a bucket*.

Training a horse's body, mind, and habit of obedience to gallop perfect circles with no correction or support is a complicated and lengthy journey. The milestones of that journey are the same as the steps along the way for horses who will participate in jumping, dressage, roping, barrel racing, reining, or competitive trail events.

First the horse has to know you're there. He has to show up. Once the foundations of relationship and a vocabulary that permits communication are established the horse has to learn what you mean by gallop, lope, or canter. The concept of right and left leads comes later as does steering, proper frame and balance, and staying on the right path.

As my journey with Christ moves forward the obvious and sharp corrections become less frequent and more subtle. Horses know they are doing right when there is no pressure to do something else. The same is true for New Creations in Christ.

The hands of God are merciful and His touch full of grace. The reins in His hands direct, correct, and support those whom He loves. Learn to seek and love the moments where God's supporting rein reminds you to watch where you're going or lifts what is falling down. Recognize that feeling no pressure at all usually means you are on the right path and traveling well.

Correction is used to make perfect, not to punish.

> *"For whom the* LORD *loves He corrects, Just as a father the son in whom he delights." – Proverbs 3:12*

With a proper foundation and method of communication the journey of sanctification moves from constant direction and correction to one where the Holy Spirit within directs rather than the Holy Spirit without. Transformative relationship changes what is inside.

As the journey of horse and rider progresses, observers should find it increasingly more difficult to tell where the rider and horse work independently as the level of spiritual and physical unity grows. As time goes on the rider gives very few conscious cues and the horse makes very few conscious responses. They simply move together.

Are your feet still on the right path or have you wandered off into the weeds of distraction or temptation? What does your spirit tell you? Do you feel God's subtle pressure of correction or are you moving freely in unison with no division between your spirit and His?

When a horse is unsure it will move something to see where the boundary lies. As faith increases in the One in charge of the relationship these moments of insecurity become less frequent.

The responsibility to maintain the relationship with a horse is yours. The state and condition of your relationship with

Jesus Christ is also your responsibility.

~

"And you will seek Me and find Me, when you search for Me with all your heart." – Jeremiah 29:13

The peace of the Garden of Eden is not a physical place we seek; it is a place of relationship, of new beginnings, of peace and joy. It is the spiritual union of humanity and divinity, the melding of the Spirit of God and the spirit of a man or woman. It is the journey of joy.

Horses do not seek a physical place. They need relationship with a worthy leader, a new beginning, peace and joy. A horse is elevated beyond its natural state by relationship with a person who loves and is loved by Jesus Christ.

The Garden of Eden was a place of leisure, fellowship, security, peace, and love. There is no place to find such perfect delights in this world, but it is possible to create something very similar through transformative relationship.

A horse seeks out his master because that is where he finds his place of leisure, fellowship, security, peace, and love.

Perfection

"My worth to God in public is what I am in private." – Oswald Chambers

Christian perfection is not the condition of being without blemish. Christian perfection is a journey of faith that produces the sweet fruit of joy without end and knows a peace that passes all understanding. Perfection is the abundance of faith, the absence of fear, and a heart, mind, body, and soul that acts in one accord with the Holy Spirit.

The journey to perfection is the journey of sanctification. The journey will not end until we join Jesus Christ in a future glorified form. Each step toward our goal is testimony of the state of our relationship with Jesus and produces more and sweeter fruit.

Private Practice Predicts Public Performance

The truth of your private life with Christ is displayed in what you do publicly. It is only possible to serve God openly if you serve Him privately first. Being successful in any venture depends on what habits or foundations have been chiseled into strength of character, physical fitness, or mental agility during private moments of practice and preparation.

> *"But you, when you pray, go into your room, and when you have shut your door, pray to your Father who is in the secret place; and your Father who sees in secret will reward you openly." – Matthew 6:6*

Unlike horse shows or other competitions, God evaluates what we do in private rather than what we do in public. Public failure to focus or offer obedience to our Master originates in the private moments we share – or fail to share – with the Holy Spirit.

There has never been a champion in anything who did not commit hours, days, and years of his or her life to practice. The violin virtuoso, figure skater, golfer, magician, pianist, sculptor, carpenter, scientist, writer, chess master, tennis player, or equestrian who earns the title of Champion after winning a competition spends only a tiny fraction of their time in front of crowds.

Excellent performance is the result of excellent practice. The chance of laying down a winning reining pattern at the Futurity is slim to none without having left hundreds of perfect maneuvers at home in the practice arena. Ice skaters who can't land a triple axel at home better not count on landing one during the Nationals. If you only catch one steer out of twenty you probably won't win a check at the big roping next month.

Some folks don't ride their horses for months and then jump them into a trailer and head out to the show or a barrel race. Some come home with ribbons. And some folks win the lottery. Most folks who buy tickets take a 100% loss.

Too many horse owners haul to horse shows hoping they will make it through their classes without a wreck. If you and your horse aren't successful at home why expect something different elsewhere?   How often does God see you at home working on perfecting your focus on Him and listening for His voice? If you're never around for God to speak to in private, why would you expect Him to speak to you elsewhere?

Faith is a spiritual muscle that only strengthens when tested. The Holy Spirit interprets and individualizes God's promises to each of His children in private. Faith expands with each and every promise kept. Faith grows each time we experience the private, present, willing, and personal faithfulness of God.

Christians rich in private time with God learn to view the world through a lens honed by the tutelage of the Spirit. Confidence in God's power, promise, and presence creates a confidence that He is beside you in any crisis or trial. Days, months, and years spent walking with Christ prepare you to face anything the world throws at you without fear. Indeed, what is there to be afraid of? You walk with God. In the here and now He is omnipresent. He is real, familiar, and forever.

Prayer is conversation with God. Prayer may be quiet, active, restful, powerful, conversational or a monologue. Prayer is a habit created and perfected in private so that it may be carried into the world as naturally as you wear jeans or breeches, boots, or hat.

Prayer may be reflective, exhaustive, or purposeful. Simply sitting quietly in a chair dreaming about shopping, lunch, your to-do list, or reading one chapter of the Bible just to say you read it is not purposeful.

Athletes sweat. Chess players study theory and play chess. Skaters practice jumps and spins in private to build muscle memory that perfects and predicts success in competition. Pianists and other musicians drill and play. Champion horse trainers precisely plan lessons to build foundation, maintain what is already built, and to reinforce fitness of body, mind, and relationship.

Christian Horse Training is a commitment of purposefully spent private time walking in humble obedience to God's authority. Only then may you rightfully and correctly offer direction and worthy leadership to a horse. The public fruit of relationship with God or horse depends on the health of the tree that produced it in private.

Great feats of skill and depth of relationship are built on the habit and history of ensuring that every little thing is done precisely and with great skill and consistency. The path to perfection is the sum of daily practice.

Be faithful in every small simple thing and the great things will take care of themselves.

God doesn't seek to make you a perfect example of what a man could or should be, but to bring you into right relationship with Him – to deliver you through new birth as a New Creation in Christ Jesus. Perfection is showing up every time, maintaining your focus on the face of God and none other, and growing in reflexive obedience each day. Christian perfection is the journey of sanctification without detour. There is no question of ability on the path to the Narrow Gate. God makes you able, the only question is whether or not you are willing to be led.

Perfection in Christian Horse Training produces a longing in the spirit of those you encounter for the same relationship with their horse you have with yours. Humans crave what Christ offers but there's only one way to receive it. Other equestrians want a horse that reads their body language, will offer obedience without thought, and allows them to experience the miracle that is oneness with a horse. But few are willing to do what is required to build such relationship.

There is no substitute for Jesus Christ and it is not possible to be in a transformative relationship with a horse unless you are willing to be changed yourself.

Stewardship

> *"So he called him and said to him, 'What is this I hear about you? Give an account of your stewardship."* – *Luke 16:2*

People can't make a till-death-do-us-part commitment to every horse – and that's okay. Still, God holds you accountable to be good stewards over them. Everything God gifts you with, or you acquire based on your own desire or acceptance, brings with it some level of responsibility.

Every horse should benefit from the time it spends in your care. Stewardship does not endorse any particular philosophy of training or horse keeping. Good stewardship doesn't demand horse shoes or snaffle bits or endorse one feeding program over another. Good stewardship doesn't specify box stall or pasture accommodations. What it does require is attention to the health, emotional state, and needs born into every equine spirit.

Worthy leaders look for the slightest signs of anxiety, aggression, or anger in the horses they care for. Elevation in any one of these emotions signals a problem in stewardship. Stewardship lasts from the first minute until the last.

> *"Moreover it is required in stewards that one be found faithful."* – *1 Corinthians 4:2*

Reflection and Transformation

"But we all, with unveiled face, beholding as in a mirror the glory of the Lord, are being transformed into the same image from glory to glory, just as by the Spirit of the Lord." – 2 Corinthians 3:18

One of the marvels of God's creation is how humans are transformed into what they behold. What is seen most frequently often becomes the definition of normal. Whatever image you presume to be perfection, or the person you choose to obey and strive to emulate, is likely what you will become.

- The child reflects the character of her parents.

- The student reflects the character of his teacher.

- The soldier reflects the character of his commander.

- The penitent reflects the character of his priest.

- The citizen reflects the character of the society.

- The society reflects the character of the government.

- The Christian reflects the character of Christ, and

- The horse reflects the character of its master.

This tendency is true for men, nations, religions, and horses. Those with a false vision of parent, teacher, commander, priest, society, government, or Christ will assume and reflect the image of that falsehood.

The only source of truth is God's Word. Be certain that the character you reflect is that of Jesus Christ, and Him crucified. His example as Master and Lord is the blueprint for discipleship with horses. It isn't possible to reflect His character perfectly because our reflection is presently seen in an imperfect mirror.

> *"For now we see through a glass, darkly; but then face to face: now I know in part; but then shall I know even as also I am known." – 1 Corinthians 13:12*

Blessing in the Valley and the Mountain Peak

The gift of transformative relationship is finding the blessing in valleys low as well as mountains high. Enough is the feast. Today is the journey; this place and this time.

After years of declining ability I was filled with joy when I was once again able to ride toward a purpose of higher skills and training. My first week back in the saddle was a honeymoon of sorts.

I remembered my first love [Revelation 3] in the mundane tasks of saddling up, walking and lifting lightly into a jog. What exhilaration! I had been prepared never to ride again but there I was, riding Bo and *remembering*.

Bo was obedient and responsive as was Asti. I relished in the progress made in those first few rides, shining up my dusty pedestal and restoring leadership from the saddle. My horses offered their focus and obedience. I rode imaginary mountain peaks and breathed in the cool crisp air with each stride.

No one lives on the peaks of exhilaration and experience. I'm sure no exception. Week one in the saddle was amazing but week two kicked me back to reality. Somehow I had expected that being restored to physical ability would automatically return me to the same place I was as a rider and trainer before my right leg became all but useless.

I rode Bo bareback for two years because I didn't know what my body was doing to compensate for my balance and strength deficiencies. Over the past few years I picked up habits that I only discovered when Bo responded in totally unexpected ways. Whatever my body did cued the horses to respond in a similar way. My body had been doing some weird things that triggered Bo to do likewise.

The last time Bo and I entered the arena in a mounted shooting competition I was prepared to arc to the right to engage a grouping of balloons. Off we cantered toward the balloons – until Bo took a hard left and unexpectedly headed toward the far side of the pen. I collected him up and jogged out wondering what had just happened.

A friend whose opinion I respected was waiting on his horse for his next run. I rode up and asked if he'd been watching me. He had, so I asked him what happened. I knew Bo had not been disobedient, but I couldn't figure out why he'd darted off in the opposite direction from what I had in mind. My friend answered, "It looked like Bo did exactly what you asked him to. He was calm and obedient and was just doing his job."

Bo did what my body told him to do. The problem was my body was talking out of turn. I didn't know what my body was doing. I went home and did a couple of basic drills. When I asked Bo to pick up a right lead in a straight line he did. I asked him to pick up a left lead on a straight line. He did. But after two strides he switched to his right lead. We stopped. I asked again for a left lead. Bo gave it to me for less than two strides then switched back to the right. I quit asking.

I was unable to manage my balance. Bo tried to do his best but he was pretty much out there on his own. I didn't saddle him again for a long time. I couldn't tell where my seat was in a saddle but Bo's spine gave me a perfect reference point when I rode bareback.

Over the following months I learned to ride Bo bareback at all three gaits. When I returned to riding after the knee replacement I figured that all my compensatory issues would resolve themselves. Week two made it clear that I was wrong. I was a bit deflated, but my desire and commitment were undiminished. I simply had to change the focus of the program from training the horses to retraining me.

I could not figure out what I was doing. I was positive that my knees, ankles, and feet had the same angles until video evidence proved me wrong. My left side was doing what my brain told me it was, but my right side and my brain didn't appear to be speaking to one another.

Over the next weeks and months I worked to retrain my brain and find the key to balance. I forged ahead one baby step at a time. The mountains Bo, Asti and I climbed together probably looked more like molehills to the casual observer, but the journey itself is a gift, the landscape beautiful, and my companions dedicated and willing.

Getting from where you are to where you want to be isn't always a smooth trip. My passion and joy met resistance and failure. It's not easy to tell your brain it's wrong when it's perfectly content with the status quo. As each obstacle presented itself I asked, is the problem inability or unwillingness? Is the problem me or the horse?

It takes real work to undo bad habits and restore a damaged foundation. Real work. Precise work. Repetitive work. If the measure of success is based on some performance metric the work often becomes drudgery, ordinary, and passionless.

Relationship success isn't measured by any objective performance standard. Success is the quality of the journey and the sheer joy of the doing. Faith is not measured by works, and the degree of transformation in a horse/human relationship is not measured by trophies or ribbons.

What is your purpose?

There is no purpose in the life of any New Creation except relationship with Jesus Christ. We go where we are sent, in the manner and method of His direction. We are blessed and delighted to be in His presence and care.

Consider a matched pair of draft horses waiting patiently at the gate to the farmer's field. They don't look over the smooth ground before them and try to figure out how to plow it correctly. They have a master who cares for them and has proven faithful in every instance. The horses are content to stand ready until they receive direction.

The horses have shown up and patiently listen for the signal to move forward from the one who holds the reins. The horses wait to serve him willingly and well. Whatever the farmer asks the team will do. The horses don't evaluate or critique the plan or flip into fast-forward mode to judge the probable outcome.

The team of horses provides the means for the farmer to do his work. Are you as useful to God? Which do you consider more frequently, working to accomplish your goals or listening for His voice?

How many of us have prayed, "Lord grant me the vision, inspiration, and wisdom so I can accomplish this particular goal I have that will help so many people." Have you prayed for God to make you able to do something you set your mind to doing; perhaps a service for Him?

I can imagine the team of horses saying, "Master, give us the vision and power to get out and plow the cornfield for you." The response heard in reply might be, "Why do you ask me to enable you to plow the cornfield when I plan to plow the field of oats?"

Christian Horse Training is discipleship with horses. The goal of CHT is building faith through transformative relationship. Fields will be plowed along the way, but the primary goal and only element of real consequence is faith and the journey of transformation.

Delight in the Mundane

The true measure of success is found in time spent together with those you love; treasuring the moments when communication happens without conscious effort. Even in the mundane there is delight. Drudgery isn't what you do but how you look at what you do. Caring for horses and family can be a job or a joy.

Smile. Claim joy. The strength of miraculous relationship is forged on the flat repetitive plains of the every-day, not on peaks of passion. When the routine threatens your joy take smaller steps. Change the drills. Ride in the woods. Share the experience of life with the ones you cherish most.

It's easy to be distracted by what the world tells you to do and what benchmarks you should use to determine success. What if I'm never as good a rider or trainer as I used to be? Asti is the only one of our horses who knew me back when I was *able*. She is the most well trained horse in the barn but not the one I am closest to.

I will be content to perform the most basic exercises in unison of spirit and relationship with Bo, Swizzle, or Shiner if that is all I am able to do. The only element that prevents any of our horses from doing great things is my ability to prepare them. They are all bred to be champions, but their value and worth to me is based on nothing more than who they are *in relationship to me*.

Jesus Christ is well aware of your genealogy. Like horses, our Lord is not impressed by what you look like, how much money you have, who your family is, and who you know.

All that matters is who you are *in relationship to Him*.

The journey continues. Enough is as good as a feast. Each day spent in the company of my Savior and my horses is a gift.

The blessing above all other blessings is the journey of transformative relationship – the walk itself – moment by moment and year after year. Remember, the *process* of sanctification, of continuing transformation, is *enough*. It is a feast. It is a journey of joy beyond description and delivers a peace that passes understanding.

At the end of this journey is heaven itself.

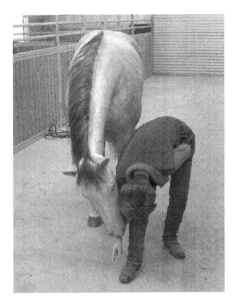

Bo

ABOUT THE AUTHOR

A former business consultant and motivational speaker, Christian writer Lynn Baber exchanged the board room for the barn at the end of the 1980's. Her success as an equine professional includes achievement as a World and National Champion horse breeder and trainer, judge, Certified Equine Appraiser, and expert witness.

The primary message of Lynn's work is "Faith over Fear." She openly shares lessons learned from personal experience with domestic violence, hopelessness, serious family illness, failure, perseverance, and success.

Lynn says the messages she delivered as a motivational speaker were absolutely correct, but today she knows where these principles are found in the Bible. She teaches Christian Horse Training as a brand of Amazing Grays Ministry. Whether shared in print, in person, or in the round pen working with troubled horses, the message will always be God's faithfulness and grace.

Lynn and her husband Baber (Larry) share the barn in Weatherford, Texas, with their horses, dogs, and cats.

OTHER TITLES BY LYNN BABER:

Amazing Grays, Amazing Grace: Pursuing right relationship with God, horses, and one another (2010)

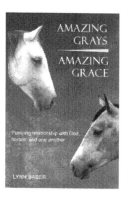

A scripturally based master class in worthy leadership using the relationship between human and horse as a mirror of that between God and man. God's promise is eternal life. The vehicle is His amazing grace, delivered by two gray quarter horses.

What readers say:

"A few books are scholarly and informative. Others are entertaining and sweet. Rarely do you see the two combined in one but Baber pulls this off". – George D.

"If you are a Christian or a horse person or both Get it. Read it. Share it. At times I felt as though it was written just for me" - LAS

"Eternal truths from a horse trainer." – Tenney S.

"I have read all three of her books and waiting for more! Don't miss "Rapture and Revelation, it's life changing!" – Jane C.

He Came Looking for Me - A true story of hope and redemption, (2011)

How does the story of an unwanted horse prove God's promise of a mansion in heaven? A modern day Black Beauty, Shiner shares his true story proving that no matter how hopeless your circumstances appear, God's promises are true. The amazing grays are back again as life in the barn continues.

What readers say:

"For those who are Christians, horse lovers or not, this is also a great book for encouragement. Several passages had me in tears as they were just what I needed to hear." – Sarah F.

"He Came Looking For Me" is a refreshing, delightful and insightful book. Lynn Baber draws you into a "Looking Glass" so to speak...where you see, feel, and experience the connection and relationship between humans and horses." – Mary K.M.

"It is a book that offers hope, demonstrates love, and shows the reader the value of faith."- Sonja B.

Rapture and Revelation - Welcome to the End Time, (2012)

The King is coming. This is the End Time and a choice must be made between God and Not God. Why do you believe what you believe? Many Christians have been shocked to discover that the "jesus" they know is not the Son of God. Simple and direct, with loads of scriptural citations upon which the message is founded.

All titles are available in paperback, Kindle, and EPUB reader formats.

Visit Lynn Baber on Amazon.com, Smashwords, and the ministry store.

Contact Information:

www.AmazingGraysMinistry.com
www.ChristianHorseTraining.com
www.LynnBaber.com

36142642R00165

Made in the USA
Middletown, DE
25 October 2016